The Structure of the
Book of Job

CLAUS WESTERMANN

The Structure of the Book
of Job

A Form-Critical Analysis

translated by
Charles A. Muenchow

FORTRESS PRESS   **PHILADELPHIA**

This book is a translation of the second edition of *Der Aufbau des Buches Hiob,* copyright © 1977 by Calwer Verlag, Stuttgart, Germany.

Biblical quotations from the Revised Standard Version of the Bible, copyright 1946, 1952, © 1971, 1973 by the Division of Christian Education of the National Council of the Churches of Christ in the U.S.A., are used by permission.

Library of Congress Cataloging in Publication Data

Westermann, Claus,
   The structure of the Book of Job.

   Translation of Der Aufbau des Buches Hiob.
   1. Bible. O.T. Job—Criticism, interpretation, etc. I. Title.
BS1415.2.W4513   1981   223'.106   80–2379
ISBN 0–8006–0651–5

8010I80   Printed in the United States of America 1–651

Contents

Preface to the Second German Edition

The first edition of my investigation into the structure of the Book of Job has long been out of print. In the meantime, inquiry into the Book of Job has continued; research since 1956 has produced a host of varied works in the field. Until now, however, there has been neither wholesale refutation of nor measurable advance on the form-critical approach of my initial study. It is hoped that this new edition might serve to raise once again the question regarding the underlying structures of the Book of Job.

At the base of my investigation lies the simple recognition that in the Old Testament human suffering has its own peculiar language and that one can understand the structure of the Book of Job if one has first understood this language, namely, the language of lamentation. As lamentation, which is suffering expressed in speech, gets developed along the three axes which determine human existence in general—the self in isolation, the self over against other human beings, and the self over against God—so the poet of the Book of Job presents the suffering of Job through the three representations of this threefold aspect of human existence: Job himself, the friends of Job who become his enemies, and God. This basic recognition, garnered from the structure of lamentation, provides the key that unlocks the meaning of the entire Book of Job, not only those parts which contain Job's laments, but also the whole polarity of lamentation and praise out of which the dramatic dialogue arises.

There remain many questions needing further research. The traditions reworked in the Book of Job are still in need of fundamental investigation, the individual forms of speech need comprehensive examination, and the wisdom elements require more precise determination and clarification. Developments in the history of religions also suggest the need for further comparative studies and a fresh examination of possible interconnections.

Preface to the English Edition

This study is based on the simple insight that in the Bible suffering has a language all its own and that one must understand the language of lament if one is to understand the Book of Job. As the lament, the language of suffering, encompasses three dimensions of human existence—being a self, being together with others, and being before God—so the author of the Book of Job pictures Job's suffering in the three persons who embody it: Job, the friends of Job who in turn become his enemies, and God. This insight, derived from the structure of the Book of Job, affords the key to understanding this remarkable book, whose power has remained undiminished over thousands of years.

I am grateful to Fortress Press for making my work on Job available to the English-speaking world. This first English edition is based on the second German edition published by Calwer Verlag in 1977, which also included Jürgen Kegler's survey of the literature on Job since 1956, the year of the first German edition.

21 August 1980   CLAUS WESTERMANN

Translator's Note

This translation aims at readability for the nonspecialist in biblical studies. In keeping with this, biblical citations follow the Revised Standard Version (RSV) wherever possible; where Professor Westermann's understanding of a verse differs from that reflected in the RSV, the citation is a translation of the author's own wording, cross-checked against the Hebrew. The use of quotation marks within a biblical citation identifies an emendation in the Hebrew text accepted by Professor Westermann. References to biblical versification follow the RSV throughout; where the Hebrew may differ (as frequently in Psalms and consistently in chap. 41 of the Book of Job), the corresponding Hebrew versification is given in brackets. All Hebrew words are transliterated, though vocalization is included where a particular grammatical form or a specific occurrence of a Hebrew word is involved.

1

The Literary Genre of the
Book of Job

Is the Book of Job to be classified as wisdom literature? Until now this question has been answered predominantly in the affirmative, yet recently several voices have been raised in opposition.[1] Essentially they contend that so far as literary form is concerned the Book of Job is utterly unique.[2] The whole question of literary form would become significant only if the judgment concerning literary classification were to have a decisive effect upon the exegesis of the book. Historically this seems not to have happened; at least interpreters of Job have not argued much about this matter of literary classification.[3] In fact, however, the categorizing of Job as wisdom literature has clearly exerted a pervasive, perhaps even controlling, influence upon nineteenth- and twentieth-century exegesis. This becomes apparent at one particular point: most modern interpretations proceed on the assumption that the Book of Job deals with a "problem." For example, Theodore H. Robinson writes: "The subject of this poem is the most serious problem that has ever troubled the human mind."[4] In the words of Johannes Lindblom, the poet "discusses, upon the occasion of the misfortune of Job, the problem of divine retribution and of the justice of God."[5] Sellin and Rost say that Job treats the problem "How is the suffering of a just man to be reconciled with the existence of a just God?"[6] This basic proposition—that the Book of Job deals with a problem—reflects a prior decision regarding the "meaning" of the Book of Job, a decision which cannot help but exert a controlling influence upon the exegesis of the book.[7] However, one cannot avoid noticing that those interpreters who agree on the basic proposition that the Book of Job deals with a problem obviously disagree on just what that problem is. Furthermore, the history of interpretation shows no progress on this crucial question as to the nature of the problem. Regarding this decisive question Kuhl confirms, "The history of Job research simply does not reveal clearly recognizable and distinctive stages."[8] Might not this lack of progress indicate that the widely shared assumption that the Book of Job deals with a problem needs now to be reconsidered? Does the Book of Job really address a problem—perhaps even several problems—that can be expressed in the form of a question such as that formulated by Sellin and Rost? But if the Book of Job does in fact deal with a question, then surely it is not a theoretical question but an existential question.[9] This is clear from the conclusion of the book, which, as more recent interpreters generally agree, does not offer a conceptual or theoretical answer.[10]

To inquire about something is to make of it an object. Whatever the thing may be, inquiry concerning it involves the attempt to grasp it conceptually. If the thing in question is suffering, or, more precisely, the suffering of a just man, then in a certain sense that just man becomes an object—the object of thought.

Existential questions are put differently. For example, the existential question "Why must I suffer?" does not arise because a person thinks about his own suffering and makes it an object of thought. It arises out of the suffering as such, as a kind of direct reaction to it; it is a *reactio* arising in response to a previous *actio*. There are various kinds of reaction to pain and suffering, such as screaming or remedial action. When the reaction is verbal we call it a lament. The question "Why must I suffer?" is a lament, insofar as it is an existential question. To be sure, it can go on to become a theoretical question, but by then it is only a derivative question.

The lament is widely attested in the Book of Job; in fact, it dominates the book. Fundamentally the book treats an existential question. Therefore interpretation of the Book of Job must take as its starting point the existential question, in other words, the lament. It cannot take as its point of departure some problem, such as "the problem of suffering." A lament is something fundamentally different from a treatment of the problem of suffering. A lament does not arise out of mournful reflection on suffering—what some interpreters call elegaic thought. On the contrary, a lament is an existential process which has its own structure. This has far-reaching consequences for exegesis. Where it is supposed that, in the lament sections, the poet of the Book of Job is dealing with the problem of suffering, Job's being a case in point, the interpreter will be inquiring into the thoughts of any given section (e.g., chaps. 3 or 30) and their interconnections. However, where it is seen that the poet is not merely using the style of the lament in order to express his thoughts after the manner of songs of lamentation, but that these are real laments, the interpreter will have to examine to what extent and how in these sections the lament develops along the lines of its own forms and in consonance with its own rules. In the Book of Job the poet does not string together mournful reflections whose interconnections we can figure out by our logic. On the contrary, in his laments he stands in a tradition of fixed forms whose richness and impressive design can be appreciated only against the background of the whole history of the lament in the Old Testament, from whence these forms derive.[11]

What has been said so far applies to only one component of the Book of Job, not to the book as a whole. Hence one might argue that, while it may well have significance for the lament sections of the book, it is inconsequential for interpretation of the book as a whole; the whole—or in any case the chief part—is dialogue, a dialogue which has the character of a discussion, and the Book of Job as a whole therefore is still a discussion of a problem. Here one must ask, though, whether it really is a discussion; it is certainly *not* a discussion in the sense in which we customarily understand the word. Rather, it is a disputation, and that is something quite different. Köhler has clearly delineated the distinguishing characteristics of the disputation and its affinity to courtroom speech.[12] Lindblom has emphasized that the manner of speech in a disputation is essentially different from that in an "objective" discussion.[13] A disputation is a forensic process; the parties involved do not discuss a problem, but rather argue a matter before a court of law.

This clarification does not close the matter, however, for it does not yet adequately explain the dialogue form in the Book of Job.[14] Indeed, the friends come to Job neither to have a discussion with

him nor to carry on a disputation; they come to console him. Here I
agree with Bentzen that the dialogue form in the Book of Job is
simply the dialogue of consolation, even though from the very
beginning consolation is transformed into disputation.[15] The
intended consolation misfires and is replaced by disputes, as we
shall see later. This dialogue section (chaps. 4–27) is framed by the
laments of Job (chaps. 3 and 29–31) which stand outside the disputation and are strictly laments, lacking any sort of address to the
friends. This means that the dialogue stands *within* the lament. The
lament is there both before and after the dialogue with the friends;
it has both the first and the last word. Out of Job's lament, however, a new "dialogue" arises; disillusioned with his friends, Job
turns directly to God and demands an answer. And the Book of Job
reports that God did answer. God's answer to Job (chaps. 38–41)
clearly has—at least in part—the character of a disputation. Therefore disputational speech connects the characters of the drama in
this fashion

Friends ⇌ Job ⇌ God

with the dialogue between Job and God following after that
between the friends and Job, even though the foundations for it
were laid already at the beginning. This sequence is necessitated by
the fact that Job has to appeal to a higher court when his friends
refuse to hear his case. In the decisive places, especially at the end
of chap. 31, Job's appeal to God employs the language of a legal
proceeding. The whole process, whose contours are thus sketched
out, in no way resembles the character of a discussion about some
theme or problem. What is presented is rather a legal proceeding
terminating in a decision.[16] The legal decision demanded by Job is
preceded by a disputation. Because the chief element on Job's side
of this disputation is the lament, God's decision is at the same time
the answer to Job's lament. The most important element in the
speeches of the friends is something quite different. They alone
advance arguments in their speeches; in Job's speeches—except for
one at the end, as we shall see—the lament stands in the place of the
argument. This incongruity between the speeches of the friends and
the speeches of Job is the most noticeable and also the most impor-

tant structural clue in the book. Disputational speech is common to all three parties, as we have seen; that is to say, for all three something is being contested. However, the disputational speech in any given instance serves only as the introduction. The resemblance between the speeches of Job and those of the friends is purely superficial: each speech is introduced by a personal address, upon which follows a speech about something. The friends in every case present arguments, their chief argument being the doctrine about the fate of the transgressor. In place of the arguments, however, Job inserts a lament. (In only one place in the dialogue section do thesis and antithesis stand in clear juxtaposition: in chap. 21, the last speech of the second cycle of discourse, Job sets his thesis over against that of the friends regarding the fate of the transgressor; only here does Job directly contest the doctrine of retribution.) It is this incongruity which gives the book its peculiar drama. Throughout the whole dialogue section there is this juxtaposition of doctrine and lament. The doctrine, which comes directly out of tradition but is now rigidified, stands over against the burning lament, which arises directly out of an existential anguish. The lament finds no hearing and elicits no consolation; the doctrine ricochets off the reality of pain. Thus the disputation must run its course without resolution; only the higher court can decide.

However, Job had already turned to this higher court—cryptically, to be sure—*before* the onset of the disputation. A straight line leads from this opening accusation against God in chap. 3 to Job's summoning of God at the end of chap. 31. The bracketing of the dialogue section (chaps. 4–27) by the element of lament, in which Job turns directly to God, corresponds substantively to the incongruity noted within the dialogue section. There is then only one way to see the whole of the Book of Job: the encompassing confrontation is that between Job and God, while within this confrontation stands the one between the friends and Job. What happens between the friends and Job begins with the first speech of Eliphaz (chap. 4) and ends with Job's answer to the third speech of Eliphaz (chap. 23; on chaps. 24–27 see below). What happens between Job and God begins with the lament in chap. 3 and ends with God's answer to Job's final, summarizing lament in chaps. 29–31, which climaxes in Job's summoning of God

(31:35–37). This divine-human interaction is never totally inter-rupted in the middle section (chaps. 4–27) but rather is continued in Job's laments, which are components of his speech in the dialogue section. When finally Job turns irrevocably away from his friends, he once again confronts God alone. Chapters 4–27 are therefore in no way the whole; to be sure, they are the longest part, but they are a part of the whole. One can depict the whole something like this:

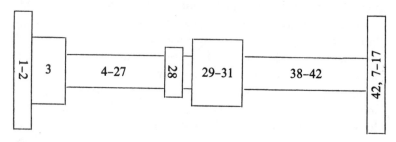

The whole, then, is neither a disputation nor a dialogue. What is depicted is an event involving three partners or parties: Job, the friends, and God. Thus the Book of Job is really a drama.[17] Of course, it is not a drama in the firmly fixed literary sense the word has for us now, but it is a drama in the original sense of the word. The poet presents an occurrence, an event. He presents it not, or at least not only, in the style of a narrative or a report. Instead he works an event into the framework of a narrative. This event com-mences with a lament, upon which an act of consolation is sup-posed to follow. The consolation, however, turns into disputation. This disputation breaks off without resolution, at which point the lament resumes and leads up to a summoning of God. God answers, and Job submits to God. This is the event depicted by the Book of Job.

The event is fitted into the framework of a narrative. What sig-nificance does this narrative have for the whole?[18] As we said above, the poet depicts an event, one which happens to a definite, real, living human being with a specific name and living in a partic-ular place. In like manner, his three friends are not just any sort of characters, but men with names and personalities. The poet presents a true story about real people. Now this does not mean that Job and his friends are historical in our sense of the word, namely, that their existence can be established on the basis of documentary evidence. However, it does mean that Job is not just an instance in which something is to be demonstrated.[19] On the contrary, Job was a real person, a unique individual.

The narrative framework of the Book of Job is necessary in order to make all this clear at the outset. The narrative framework is in no way superfluous to the book as a whole; it simply *must* be there. This is further established, in my mind, by the fact that the poet of the "drama" chose to employ a story already current in the tradition of his people. He did not want to invent a figure; he speaks of a man who had already lived. That this traditional story does not agree in places with the event which the poet depicts in lament, disputation, and divine response is actually a sign of "authenticity"—in a sense other than the literary one. The poet lets us recognize, and *wants* us to recognize, that he is appropriating an earlier, long since fixed story.[20]

If one looks closely, one sees that this is the same process which frequently shows up in the historical books of the Old Testament, only in reverse: a participant in a story has a song placed on his lips, but in such a way that we can still clearly recognize that song and story each has a different point of origin, that each stands in its own line of tradition, and that both have here been deliberately fused together. Examples of this include the song of praise which a king sings at the high point of his reign (2 Sam. 22 = Ps. 18), the lament of an ill king (Isa. 38), the lament of a childless woman (1 Sam. 1), the song of the prophet Jonah, and the songs of the community in Chronicles, which are constructed out of psalms. The Song of Hannah (1 Sam. 2) is probably the example closest to Job. What is framework in the Book of Job is here the real focus of interest, namely, the narrative of the birth of a child. A song is inserted into this narrative, but it does not really fit. One would have expected a song of thanksgiving at this juncture in the story, but instead one finds a descriptive song of praise which is clearly recognizable as a secondary insertion. Thus the song, which one well knows was frequently sung and familiar to many, is here placed in the mouth of a particular person on a specific occasion. Moreover, it matters neither to the author nor to the hearers that the song does not quite fit in with the story. The reverse situation is found in the Book of Job: the story is affixed to the poem as its framework. This gives the poem its character as an event; the one lamenting in the poem is a real person. That two constructs of different origin are hereby joined is not concealed, nor is it meant to be concealed. One must therefore differentiate between the Job-poem proper and the narrative framework, but one must also constantly keep in mind that the Job-poem cannot be thought of apart from the framework.

However, the Job-poem proper must now be even more precisely defined. Can one be more explicit about the nature of the event presented? In my opinion, Bentzen has here suggested a whole new interpretation which can open the way to a shift in one's overall view of the Book of Job. Bentzen starts out from Lindblom's observation to the effect that the closest religio-historical parallel to the Book of Job is the Babylonian poem "I will serve the Lord of Wisdom." As Bentzen says,

> "I will serve the Lord of Wisdom" . . . is in reality a psalm, a combined psalm of lamentation and of thanksgiving, which has certainly been used in the temple-cult. . . . The parallel poems in dialogue form are only a further development of the situation of the psalm of lamentation and its forms. . . . *The dialogue is a "dramatization" of the psalm of lamentation,* more accurately, of the "prayers of the accused," placed in the frame of a narrative.[21]

Bentzen then inquires into the background of the origin of this process of dramatization in the Book of Job and finds a possible answer in the poem itself:

> According to the framework of the book, the narrative, the friends of Job arrive to *console* Job. Is it not probable that this feature has been borrowed from reality? . . . So the dialogue in a natural way grows under the hand of the poet, and in this situation he is able to use the many forms, especially of psalms of lamentation, which he displays in his lyrics.[22]

If one looks closely one sees here two different explanations. To start with the second, the dialogue is conditioned simply by the situation of consolation. Because the speeches of the friends are anything but consoling, this straightforward explanation of the dialogue form has heretofore never been seriously entertained. Now admittedly the speeches offer no consolation. However, the conclusion generally drawn from this fact is open to question. Simply because the speeches of the friends, who had come to console Job, were not actually consoling, it does not follow that the dialogue form has nothing to do with the process of consolation. On the contrary, the *situation* of consolation remains in effect: Job *remains* the lamenter, and nothing alters the fact that the proper role for the friends, to the very end, was that of offering consolation. This is no mere hypothesis; it is repeatedly and clearly stated by Job himself:

As for you, you whitewash with lies;
  worthless physicians are you all. (13:4)

Are the consolations of God too small for you,
  or the word that deals gently with you? (Eliphaz, 15:11)

I have heard many such things;
  miserable comforters are you all. (16:2)

I could strengthen you with my mouth,
  and the solace of my lips would assuage your pain. (16:5)

Listen carefully to my words,
  and let this be your consolation. (21:2)

How then will you comfort me with empty nothings?
  There is nothing left of your answers but falsehood. (21:34)

How you have helped him who has no power!
  How you have saved the arm that has no strength!
How you have counseled him who has no wisdom,
  and plentifully declared sound knowledge!
With whose help have you uttered words,
  and whose spirit has come forth from you? (26:2–4)

As the citation from 15:11 clearly shows, not only Job but also the friends know well that the proper office of the latter is consolation. In my opinion the beginning of the first of the friends' speeches displays the same realization, for how else would one understand the fact that this speech follows directly upon Job's lament? In any case, Job does not open chap. 3 with a disputation speech; he laments, and furthermore, his lament contains no trace of an attack on the friends. What else besides a word of consolation should follow such a lament? No speech by a friend is so amicable, reserved, and sympathetic to Job as the beginning of the first speech of Eliphaz; the properly intended consolation still sounds forth here. Contrary to his own intention, Eliphaz's word of consolation leads to disputation.

There is yet another reason why it has never before been seen, or at least conceded, that the dialogue between the friends and Job has grown out of the situation of consolation. We are accustomed to regard consolation as a one-way process. In other words, we understand by "consolation" simply a consoling or comforting word. However, the real process of consolation is a dialogue. In such a process it is essential that the sufferer or mourner be led to speak amid his suffering; thus the consoling words assume the character of an answer to the lament. What it comes down to is that a repeated exchange of words belongs to the very essence of the process of consolation. In real situations of consolation—as experience demonstrates thousandfold—it almost never happens that the sufferer speaks only once and the consoler replies only once. It is furthermore essential to the process of consolation that the one doing the lamenting be allowed to express himself. Therefore an attitude of reservation is incumbent upon the consoler in such a conversation, whereas the one doing the lamenting has the right to be expansive in his lament. The particular structure of the dialogue in the Book of Job shows precisely this arrangement. The sufferer speaks first (chap. 3); Job's speeches are usually longer than those of the friends; above all, the friends allow Job to respond after each individual utterance on the part of one of them (i.e., AB, AC, AD, AB, AC, AD, etc.; not ABCD, ABCD). Job's speeches remain laments to the very end (23:2); instead of disputations, he expected consolation from his friends right up to the end—even though in vain (21:34).

In terms of its content, therefore, the whole dialogue section is actually consoling conversation. Our arguments advanced above confirm Bentzen's supposition. However, in one place in this consoling conversation, namely, where the friends were obligated to extend comforting words to Job, disputation has instead intruded—disputation corresponding to that found in the realm of jurisprudence and finally leading up to an indictment. Köhler has expounded upon this aspect of the dialogue section.[23] But now—as we have already indicated—the two sides of this disputation are not congruent. On the one hand, the speeches of Job contain laments rather than arguments, even though introduced as disputational speech. On the other hand, the disputation is encompassed by the lament (chaps. 3 and 29–31). From Job's perspective it appears as though the lamenter is assailed by his friends and left in the lurch when his friends were supposed to stand by him. So Job turns on his friends and accosts them. Bentzen's other explanation applies to this aspect of the dialogue section, namely, that we have here a dramatized lament. In support of this view, Bentzen refers to Ps. 41:9[10] and 51:11–13[13–15], in which the lamenter laments that his friends have become enemies to him. It is true that the same procedure is intimated here which is widely developed in the Book of Job. However, this does not yet explain the presence of the dialogue form. Fortunately, among the so-called individual lament psalms there is a small group in which the transition from lamentation to disputational speech is already carried out on the part of the lamenter—even if only in suggestive, stylized fashion. These are the psalms in which the lamenter addresses his opponents in such words as:

> O men, how long shall my honor suffer shame?
>   How long will you love vain words, and seek after lies?
> But know that . . . (Ps. 4:2[3])

> Depart from me, all you workers of evil;
>   for the Lord has heard the sound of my weeping. (Ps. 6:8[9])[24]

In these places there really is a dramatizing of the lament! These cases in Psalms are not hard to explain. First of all, a very considerable expansion shows up at the place of the third component of the lament (viz., the indictment of the enemies) in the genre of the individual lament.[25] In this regard, sometimes the evildoers step so strongly to the fore that they dominate the whole psalm. Corresponding to the degree to which this happens, the proper confrontation—namely, that between the lamenter and God—is overshadowed by the confrontation between the lamenter and his friends. The result, on the one hand, is a very extensive discourse *about* the enemies, which actually breaks through the genre of the lament;[26] on the other hand, the discourse leaps over into an address directed *to* the enemies. Psalm 4:2[3] could stand unaltered in a speech of

Job! The direct address of the friends in the speeches of Job has its parallels in the address of the enemies in the individual lament psalms already cited. In both places, this element of address arises out of the lament and remains encompassed by the lament. Of course, a considerable gulf separates those few verses from the individual lament psalms and the speeches of Job; however, a real correspondence exists with regard to the genre of speech and the situation.

The formal elements of the Book of Job have thus been determined. The dialogue is supposed to become a consoling conversation in which the speech of the one partner would have to be lament and that of the other consolation. Controversy crops up in the place of the consolation offered by the friends, and this leads to arguments. On Job's side, the lament remains the chief component. However, alongside the lament there must now appear opposition to the friends, with the result that the whole comes to be depicted as a disputation. Nevertheless, this disputation, which has come together out of different elements, remains encompassed by the lament (chaps. 3 and 29–31), which has the first and the last word. Direct address of the friends is missing in this lament. However, the secret third partner in the conversation *is* addressed in the lament, namely, God. The whole ends with the summoning of God at the end of the last lament (31:35–37). The controversy is thereby taken to the higher court. Only Job and God are left to face one another. The dramatizing of the lament now demands that some sort of an answer be given in response to Job's summons, whereby the word which will resolve the controversy will be spoken. This whole happening is placed within the framework of a narrated story. With this dramatizing of the lament, the poet has not constructed an illustrative case but has reported an event which befell a real human being.

The three partners in this event, or drama, correspond to the three parts of the lament.[27] Thereby the explanation of the whole as a dramatizing of the lament receives still further confirmation. This determination of the formal elements of the Book of Job is of vital importance for the exegesis of the book. Each individual sentence of the book stands in a twofold context. First of all, it stands in the respective context of a speech by Job, by one of the friends, or by God. At the same time, however, it is also a part of the depicted event, which is itself composed of the formal elements pointed out above. The character of this event is not to be ascertained in the way attempted by most up to now, namely, by pursuing a line of thought which supposedly penetrates the whole Book of Job. On the contrary, it is to be determined only by way of placing each individual sentence in the context proper to it in the respective genres of speech. This means that a line from Job's lament must be seen in the context of the total lament throughout the whole book, that a line in praise of God must be seen against the background of all the sentences praising God, and that a single disputation must be viewed in the context of the whole of the disputation. Allied with this is the fact that each individual genre of speech must be investigated throughout the whole book. Thus it is important just *where* an avowal of trust stands, *where* one part of a lament dominates while another part is totally lacking, *where* and *how* wishes and petitions are inserted, and *how* the distribution is made between references to personal matters and remarks of a substantive sort. This sort of questioning opens up avenues and perspectives which simply could not come to light through an inquiry into the book's course of thought. Only in this way can one come to recognize the poem's structure, which has grown out of living genres of speech and not out of abstract thinking.[28] In the chapters which follow we will consider these genres, the formal elements in the composition.

NOTES

1. In my opinion the soundest and most important objection has been raised by Paul Volz (*Das Buch Hiob,* Schriften des Alten Testaments 3/2 [Göttingen, 1911], pp. 25-26 ["Hiobs Klage kein Lehrgedicht"]). Subsequent defenders of the same view include Artur Weiser, *Das Buch Hiob,* Das Alte Testament Deutsch 13 (Göttingen: Vandenhoeck & Ruprecht, 1951); Johannes Fichtner, "Hiob in der Verkündigung unserer Zeit," *Wort und Dienst,* N.F. 2 (1950): 71-89; Aage Bentzen, *Introduction to the Old Testament,* vol. 2 (Copenhagen: G. E. C. Gad, ²1952); Friedrich Baumgärtel, *Der Hiobdialog: Aufriss und Deutung,* Beiträge zur Wissenschaft vom Alten und Neuen Testament 61 (Stuttgart, 1933); and Moses Buttenweiser, *The Book of Job* (New York, 1922). All these see the lament as the chief

component of the Book of Job, and they question the classification of Job as wisdom literature on the basis of that observation. The reason this recent view of the Book of Job has not been generally accepted may well lie in the fact that the true character of the lament in the Old Testament has not been sufficiently investigated. In any case, the contemporary situation with regard to this question is ambiguous: some simply continue to classify the Book of Job as wisdom, while others cautiously question this classification. The following statement by Kuhl is characteristic of the latter tendency: "One ordinarily reckons Job as part of the wisdom literature. . . . However, the poem does not readily fit into the framework of the usual corpus of wisdom literature. . . . The poem's affinities with the poetry of the psalms, above all, its similarities to the genres of the lament and the hymn, are every bit as pronounced as its relationship to wisdom" (Curt Kuhl, "Neuere Literarkritik des Buches Hiob," *Theologische Rundschau,* N.F. 21 [1953]: 311).

2. E.g., Weiser, *Das Buch Hiob,* pp. 8-9. Cf. the remark by Kuhl: "One would therefore be well advised to see in Job an 'utterly unique poem' (Beel, p. 268), an 'independent type' (Kraeling, p. 226), which fits into none of the usual categories (Spalding, p. 290)" ("Literarkritik," pp. 311-12).

3. Kuhl's essay is the first really comprehensive presentation of the history of research on the Book of Job. Thanks are due to the author for this exceptionally painstaking survey, which has drawn together an extraordinarily immense number of individual studies.

4. Theodore H. Robinson, *The Poetry of the Old Testament* (London: Duckworth, 1947), p. 68.

5. Johannes Lindblom, *La composition du livre de Job* (Lund: C. W. K. Gleerup, 1945), p. 35.

6. Ernst Sellin and Leonhard Rost, *Einleitung in das Alte Testament* (Heidelberg: Quelle & Meyer, ⁸1950), p. 160; cf. Ernst Sellin and Georg Fohrer, *Introduction to the Old Testament,* trans. David E. Green (Nashville: Abingdon, 1968), p. 334.

7. Volz, who explicitly denies that the Book of Job deals with a problem, points this out with particular clarity in his commentary (*Das Buch Hiob,* p. 25).

8. Kuhl, "Literarkritik," p. 167.

9. Cf. Weiser, *Das Buch Hiob,* p. 9.

10. Esp. Fridolin Stier (*Das Buch Ijjob, hebräisch und deutsch* [Munich: Kosel, 1954]); cf. Weiser: "It is inappropriate . . . to try to limit the problem of Job to a theological question" (*Das Buch Hiob,* p. 9).

11. Cf. Volz: "The poet has not written a treatise but a lament" (*Das Buch Hiob,* p. 26). Baumgärtel has apparently also noticed this distinction. However, he has drawn from it the conclusion to which one is forced if one rigidly adheres to the presupposition that the Book of Job deals with a

problem: he has stricken out all those passages which he recognizes as being laments in the proper sense.

12. Ludwig Köhler, "Justice in the Gate," postscript to *Hebrew Man,* trans. Peter R. Ackroyd (London: SCM, 1956), pp. 158–63 (= "Die hebräische Rechtsgemeinde," postscript to *Der hebräische Mensch* [Tübingen: J. C. B. Mohr (Paul Siebeck), 1953], pp. 153–58).

13. Lindblom, *La composition,* pp. 40–41.

14. Cf. Kuhl, "Literarkritik," pp. 294–306.

15. Bentzen, *Introduction,* 2:174–79.

16. This interpretation of the Book of Job stands out especially clearly in the recent study by Stier; cf. my review of *Das Buch Ijjob, hebräisch und deutsch,* by Fridolin Stier, in *Eckart Jahrbuch* 25 (1955/56): 260–65.

17. Similarly Volz (*Das Buch Hiob,* p. 24), who refers to a remark by Luther which already points in the same direction; cf. also Buttenweiser, *Book of Job.*

18. Cf. Otto Eissfeldt, *The Old Testament: An Introduction,* trans. Peter R. Ackroyd (New York: Harper & Row, 1965), esp. pp. 462–66 (= *Einleitung in das Alte Testament* [Tübingen: J. C. B. Mohr (Paul Siebeck), ³1964], pp. 624–30).

19. Unfortunately, Job is described all too often as a "case" even by the most recent interpreters of the Book of Job!

20. Hermann Gunkel rightly saw this; cf. his "Hiobbuch," in *Die Religion in Geschichte und Gegenwart* (Tübingen, ²1929), vol. 2, cols. 1924–30.

21. Bentzen, *Introduction,* p. 182.

22. Ibid.

23. Köhler, "Justice," pp. 158–63.

24. Cf. also Ps. 119:115; 52:1–4[3–6]; 58:1–5[2–6].

25. Cf. Claus Westermann, "Struktur und Geschichte der Klage im Alten Testament," *Zeitschrift für die alttestamentliche Wissenschaft* 66 (1954): 44–80.

26. The lament becomes a lamenting description (ibid., p. 64).

27. See below.

28. Édouard Paul Dhorme, *A Commentary on the Book of Job,* trans. Harold Knight (London: Nelson, 1967), pp. lxi–lxii (= *Le livre de Job* [Paris, 1926], pp. xlix–l).

2

The Disputation

Ludwig Köhler has provided us with the basic description of this genre of speech in his essay "Justice in the Gate."[1] "These speeches are speeches like those which were delivered by the parties before the legal assembly. They are 'party addresses.' . . . The intention is not, as in a Platonic dialogue, to find truth in speech and counter-speech, but the presentation of a point of view already determined beforehand with such forcefulness as to persuade the listeners."[2] Unfortunately this suggestion has drawn little attention in research on the Book of Job; Kuhl now mentions Köhler in his survey,[3] and Lindblom offers a very similar interpretation of the disputation genre without referring to Köhler. Eissfeldt has accepted Köhler's insight.[4]

Köhler makes one qualification: "insofar as the content [of chaps. 3–31] does not suppress the forms which belong to the legal assembly" (p. 161). Almost all the verses he cites stand at the beginning of chapters (cf. n. 2). Both the speeches of the friends and the speeches of Job are made up of two chief elements: personal address and a substantive part consisting of arguments in the speeches of the friends and laments in the speeches of Job. However, disputational speech is common not only to the speeches of the friends and the speeches of Job; the lengthy speech by God also clearly contains such elements. On the other hand, none of the speeches is solely disputation.

A second qualification must be added. Köhler has the legal dispute begin with Job's lament in chap. 3. However, it is important when analyzing the structure of the book to realize that chap. 3 contains not the slightest polemic against the friends. Even though it is still restrained and concealed, in chap. 3 a separate controversy begins between Job and God, which finally issues in the summoning of God in 31:35-37. The controversy in the foreground—between the friends and Job—properly begins in chap. 4. The controversy between Job and God hovers in the background and gradually comes to the fore in ever sharper detail, while the controversy in the foreground progressively retreats until finally Job confronts only God. On the whole, the controversy between the friends and Job is only an interlude. With these qualifications in mind let us now turn our attention to the element of disputation as found in the speeches of the friends and of Job.

The Disputation in the Speeches of the Friends

The proportions between the personal and the substantive elements vary considerably. An initial, admittedly loose overview looks like this (personal elements in left-hand column, substantive in right-hand column):

ELIPHAZ I		BILDAD I		ZOPHAR I	
4:2-7		8:2-4		11:2-4	
	8-11	5-7		5-6a	
	12-19		8-10		7-11
(5:1-7)	5:1-7		11-19	12-14	
8	9-16	20-22			15-19
17	18-20				20
	21-26				
27					

ELIPHAZ II		BILDAD II		ZOPHAR II	
		18:2-4		20:2-5	
15:2-3			5-21	(19-21)	6-29
	14-16				
	17-35				

ELIPHAZ III

22:2–5	
6–9	
10–11	
12–20	16, 19, 20
21–28	
30b	29–30

One fact is clear from this overview. In the first cycle of discourse personal and substantive speeches are in approximate equilibrium. In the second cycle of discourse the speeches of the friends rigidify, all three employing direct address only in their respective introductions. In the third cycle of discourse—and this is significant—the emphasis in the speech by Eliphaz is totally upon direct address; purely substantive speech is almost totally lacking here. This state of affairs is conditioned, however, by the fact that Eliphaz now advances to open accusation of Job. This overview already reveals three stages of conversation in the three cycles of discourse. In the first cycle, the friends attempt to persuade Job— therefore the predominance of direct address. In the second cycle of discourse, the friends only dispute with Job and represent their point of view—throughout the sole argument about the fate of the ungodly. In the third cycle of discourse, they openly accuse Job of misdeeds against God and man.[5] This simple state of affairs seems to me to show already that the disputation between the friends and Job was originally conceived as taking place in the three cycles of discourse and that every attempt to strike out or chop up material here has failed to recognize an essential part of the structure of the Book of Job.[6] This gradation in the three cycles of discourse becomes all the more obvious if one investigates the compositional makeup of the personal addresses. Two strongly contrasting forms show up at first glance: the altercation (which in itself still allows for a considerable variety of ways of speaking) and the admonition. An admonition is usually combined with a conditioned announcement of salvation and is expressed in a form such as "Turn to God, then he will . . ." or "Turn to God, then you will . . ." (cf. 8:5–7). The admonitions are dispersed in the following way:

I	II	III
Eliphaz: 5:8, 17, 27 (21–26)	Eliphaz: —	Eliphaz: 22:21–30
Bildad: 8:5–7, 20–22	Bildad: —	
Zophar: 11:12–14 (15–19)	Zophar: —	

In the first cycle of discourse, each of the friends' speeches contains such an admonition, whereas in the second cycle admonition is totally lacking. Extensive admonition reappears in the third cycle of discourse (22:21–30), but it no longer resembles the admonition of the first cycle. In the third cycle the admonition is preceded by the unveiled accusation of Job. Eliphaz admonishes Job to return to God and renounce his misdeeds against both God (22:13–14) and man (22:6–9) even though these are misdeeds which, according to Eliphaz's own words in his first speech (4:3–4), Job could not possibly have committed. The process of intensification becomes ever more obvious. In the first cycle of discourse, the friends still consider Job's return to God a possibility, and they admonish him to do just that; in the second cycle this admonition completely ceases; in the third cycle the admonition once again appears, but now in such a way that Job can perceive it only as a bitter mocking. *All* the speeches of the friends begin with altercation:

I	II	III
Eliphaz: 4:2–6	Eliphaz: 15:2–13	Eliphaz: 22:2–5, a
Bildad: 8:2–4	Bildad: 18:2–4	rebuking question
Zophar: 11:2–4	Zophar: 20:2–5	transformed into accusation

This disputational speech, however, is by no means *one* definite form of speech. On the contrary, it includes all the forms which one can use in opposition to another. To recognize these forms, to designate them, and to differentiate between them is very difficult indeed.

The characteristic form of speech in the speeches of Eliphaz is the reproof or the rebuke. Job 4:3–6 is a censuring reproof (which is probably preceded in v. 2 by a pardoning introduction): Eliphaz

directs Job away from his present standpoint to where he really should take his stand. This initial reproof contains the concession that Job was previously God-fearing (v. 6) and that he had helped the people around him (vv. 3-4). This same Eliphaz will accuse Job of precisely the opposite in his final speech!

The second speech of Eliphaz contains a simply classical example of the reproof.[7] First of all, 15:2-3 corresponds quite closely to 4:3-6; in a manner which is still friendly, the addressee is referred to the decent, honorable standpoint he should really take. In vv. 7-11, in a more strongly polemical fashion, the one who has set himself up too high is directed back down to where he really belongs. Eliphaz rebukes the triply impudent one in where he stands vis-à-vis God (v. 8), his forebears (v. 7), and his contemporaries (vv. 9-11). The same rebuking tone can also be heard in Eliphaz's last speech in chap. 22, in the questions at the beginning ("Can a man be profitable to God? . . ." [vv. 2-4]) and in the question in v. 12 ("Is not God high in the heavens?"). At both these places, however, the reproof leads into direct accusation (vv. 5 and 13-14).[8] This reproving or rebuking speech is therefore peculiar to Eliphaz; it exhibits a very obvious intensification from the first speech to the third.

The sentence with which Bildad begins his address to Job is both more than and other than a reproof:

> How long will you say these things,
>   and the words of your mouth be a great wind? (8:2)

It means, in effect, "Now stop talking like this!" So Bildad no longer wishes to reprove Job with friendly or even with sharp words. Bildad's first utterance is already a scolding, and in the second clause ridicule is added to the scolding. Following this scolding introduction comes the disputatious question of v. 3, which typifies the reaction of both the other friends: "Does God pervert justice? Or does the Almighty pervert the right?" In this question, Bildad summarizes what he thinks Job has said about God. But in reality Job has not said that. Bildad has made a theoretical proposition out of the lament which Job has directed to God in his burning agony. To be sure, it is the proper logical deduction from what Job has said—of this there is no doubt. However, it abstracts from the lamentlike character of the words of Job, to say nothing of the fact

that the words were directed expressly to God. In his disputation, therefore, Bildad in fact does *not* reiterate the sum of Job's utterance. The question from v. 3, cited above, demands the answer no. Now Bildad confirms this no with the arguments that follow, v. 20 concluding Bildad's proof.

The beginning of the first speech of Zophar corresponds to the beginning of the first speech of Bildad. Job 11:2–3 is a scolding address to Job, upon which follows the disputing of a statement of Job. Zophar's disputation is directed against another sentence of Job's: "For you said, 'my "conduct"⁹ is pure, and I stand here clean in your eyes'" (v. 4). Here one sees how the composition of the friends' speeches has been thought through right down to the particulars. Both of the decisive points of contention with Job were already raised in Eliphaz's reproof; the other two friends pass directly to open disputation (4:7–11 corresponds to 8:3, and 4:12–17 to 11:4).

An intentional difference between the first and second cycles of discourse is also apparent with regard to this disputational form of speech. While the first cycle contains disputation of what Job had said—in concealed fashion in the speech of Eliphaz, openly in the speeches of Bildad and Zophar—such disputation is totally absent in the second cycle. This means that, in the second cycle, the friends no longer deal at all with Job's thesis; they have given up trying to refute Job on particular points. Scolding is all that remains in the personal address in the second speeches of Bildad and Zophar.

In 18:2–4 Bildad once again tries to silence Job. The second sentence here resounds like a call to order in a courtroom. In v. 3 Bildad takes precautions for his party against offensive treatment on the part of the other party; this is also a frequent occurrence in a legal dispute.¹⁰ Verse 4a is a scolding address.¹¹ Then Bildad confronts the addressee with poisonous scorn: "Shall the earth be forsaken for you, or the rock [the pillar of the earth!] be removed out of its place?" The question contains a terrible remonstrance against Job: in the way he talks of God, Job is working for the collapse of the world order. This sentence lets us see how bitterly earnest the friends were in their struggle against Job. A long, peacefully flowing description of the fate of the ungodly (vv. 5–21) rather abruptly follows these sentences of severe scolding and most arduous remon-

strance. The structure of this composition forces the conclusion that Bildad has already given up on Job and written him off. As far as Bildad is concerned, Job is already ensconced in the category of the ungodly, whose fate is sealed.

Job 20:2-3 is poorly preserved and very questionable. I read as follows:[12]

> Therefore my thoughts "storm against" me,
>   and on "this" account is my agitation within me.
> Reproof which insults me must I hear,
>   and windiness without understanding you answer me.

In v. 3 (corresponding to 18:3 in Bildad's speech) Zophar complains about Job's speeches. As far as he is concerned, the words of Job are personally offensive and substantively futile. Therefore he has a right to be upset (v. 2).[13] After this even briefer introduction, Zophar passes immediately to description of the fate of the transgressor, which likewise here encompasses the full remainder of the chapter (vv. 4-29). Not one more time is Job directly addressed.

The accusation, which is also a part of disputational speech and which we repeatedly find in connection with disputing, still needs to be viewed comprehensively.[14] In the first cycle of discourse there is as yet no direct accusation; here the friends still see both possibilities open to Job (5:1-7; 8:8-19; 11:11). Bildad goes a little beyond this point when, in 8:4, he cold-bloodedly pronounces judgment upon Job's sons. The warning of Zophar in 11:6b is an obvious indicator pointing in the direction of the accusation: God will call you to account for your sins, Job! In the second cycle of discourse, right at the beginning of the second speech of Eliphaz (15:4-6; cf. vv. 12-13), there stands an obvious accusation of Job. However, these remonstrances refer initially *only* to the current utterances of Job in the presence of his friends and not at all to his earlier life.[15] Therefore these remonstrances stand in the context of the "rebukings" which we found particularly pronounced in this chapter; it is not yet time for concluding and summarizing condemnation. The same holds true for the vehement remonstrance of Bildad in his final speech (18:4; see below), which belongs totally within the context of the scolding speech in vv. 2-4. The second speech of Zophar contains no direct accusation. The question "Do you not know this from of old . . . ?" (20:4a), which forms the bridge from the personal introduction to the description of the fate of the transgressor, is the only probable indication that what follows is meant to depict Job's own fate. Zophar already reckons Job among the transgressors.

Only in the third cycle of discourse (Eliphaz, chap. 22) does the unconcealed and final accusation come to the fore:

> Is not then your wickedness great,
>   and your iniquities without number? (v. 5)

And then, in vv. 6–9, these iniquities are enumerated in the form of direct accusation: "You have done."[16] The transgressions of which Job is accused by Eliphaz in vv. 6–9 are drawn not from observation but from tradition. Job *must* have committed all these acts, because he *is* a transgressor. *That* Job is a transgressor is concluded not on the basis of his change of fortune but on the basis of what he had said to the friends in the disputation.

This state of affairs is further confirmed by the accusation in vv. 13–14. Verse 12 recalls the majesty of God, who surveys everything from his lofty abode:

> Therefore you say, "What does God know?
>   Can he judge through the deep darkness?
> Thick clouds enwrap him, so that he does not see,
>   and he walks on the vault of heaven." (vv. 13–14)

Where and when in his speeches is Job supposed to have said this? If forced, one could take this as a rendition of Job's speech in chap. 21, but then it would be only a very remote and unclear rendition! These verses (vv. 13–14) are to be understood solely on the basis of their origin, which can here be established with certainty. If one takes a look at all the places in the individual lament psalms where the part about "the description of the ungodly" appears within the element of the lament about enemies, one clearly discerns two groups of sentences describing the wickedness of the accused: (1) The transgressors are evildoers over against humanity; they behave inhumanly. (2) The transgressors are ungodly; they do not take God seriously. This double characterization of the transgressor doubtless stands behind the twofold accusation of Job by Eliphaz in chap. 22. The second accusation, in any case, is taken directly from this motif. Baumgärtel recognized this: "Here (vv. 13–14) words and views are placed in the mouth of Job which we otherwise could not possibly discover in him. However, the words of vv. 13–14 can hardly be separated from the quite similarly worded expressions in Ps. 73:11 and 94:7."[17] Baumgärtel has correctly seen that we are here dealing with precisely this motif from Psalms.[18] However, is his resulting conclusion, namely, to strike out the verses, really necessary and to the point? When it becomes progressively more obvious in the speeches of the friends that they reckon Job among the transgressors (see below), and when the whole second cycle of discourse has the one great theme of "the fate of the ungodly," then this speech of Eliphaz with its twofold accusation is simply the necessary consequence. This speech of Eliphaz *must* come here. Eliphaz at long last openly articulates the theme of the description of the ungodly, which in fact is nothing other than one component of the genre of speech about the ungodly. The other component of this genre, namely, recitation of the fate of the ungodly, had already found expression in the earlier speeches of the friends. That Eliphaz should conceal his accusation of Job at this decisive juncture, relying totally on traditional descriptions of the ungodly, corresponds perfectly to the structure of the whole.

The Disputation in the Speeches of Job

The key to understanding the structure of the dialogues is the recognition that these speeches are composed *throughout* of both a constant element and a variable element. The underlying structure becomes apparent only when one initially disregards the constant element and concentrates on the variable one. This holds true in even greater measure for the speeches of Job than for those of the friends.

The first thing one notices in the disputation speeches of Job is a greater versatility, a fuller array of motifs, a more direct style of speech. As in the speeches of the friends, so also in the speeches of Job the three cycles of discourse display a clear and unmistakable gradation. This can be shown first of all with reference to the overall contours. In the first cycle of discourse the friends are directly addressed in a very reserved manner. The first speech begins with an apology and later contains a personal defense. The second speech even begins with a concurrence, and nowhere does it contain any attack on the friends. Obvious and developed disputational speech shows up for the first time only at the end of the first cycle of discourse (13:4-13). Here Job accuses the friends of prevaricating intervention on God's behalf.

The second cycle of discourse displays an obvious parallelism between the speeches of the friends and the speeches of Job. In both cases the element of personal address occupies only a few verses at the beginning, while talk of substantive matters fills up most of the chapters in question. The first two speeches of Job in this second cycle of discourse start out with a sharp rejection of the friends. This is coupled, in the first speech, with Job's indication that the friends fail to recognize the difference in standpoints (16:4-5): were he in their place, he could speak just as they do! In his second speech Job raises the question of whether his friends would still have the right to pass judgment on him even if their arguments were valid. Near the end of this speech Job once again entreats the friends for pity, taking up the cry of 6:28-30 in the first speech.

Only with the third speech of the first cycle of discourse did we encounter an extended personal altercation. Likewise, not until the third speech of the second cycle of discourse do we find a direct controverting of the arguments of the friends. This is Job's only real disputation speech![19] It is obviously the goal toward which the speeches of Job in both cycles of discourse lead. Here especially one sees the architectonic skill of the poet at work. The location and singularity of this speech clearly demonstrate that in the speeches of the friends and of Job we are by no means dealing with aimless ramblings and persistent repetitions. On the contrary, we discover here a structure planned even to the most minute detail and leading resolutely up to this very speech. Here—and here alone—Job radically and pointedly disputes the thesis of the friends, namely, their doctrine of the inevitability of discernible and measurable retribution. Following this speech of Job comes the final word on the part of the friends, when in his third speech Eliphaz pronounces the twofold accusation against Job. One can recognize both in the speeches of the friends and in the speeches of Job a progression leading up to this same point: the final controverting of the friends by Job (chap. 21) and the final accusation of Job by the friends (chap. 22).[20]

All this shows that the element of disputation has here come to an end. This is true even though the conclusion of the dialogue section, in its preserved form, no longer allows this fact to be clearly recognized. In chaps. 23-27 only the speech of Job at the beginning—the answer to the speech of Eliphaz in chap. 22—is clearly identifiable. But the speech in chap. 23 is not really an "answer"; as one can see at first glance, the friends are nowhere addressed directly.

This absence of direct address must be viewed against the background of the speech of Eliphaz in chap. 22. Indeed, this speech is essentially one long address to Job; it is the unveiled accusation of Job, and as such it must necessarily be presented in the form of direct address. Job does not respond to this massive, sweeping accusation (see above, p. 24). He does not even allude to it! Now he is silent. He would have to defend himself, and indeed he could do so.[21] But Job remains silent. And with his silence Job puts an end to the disputation! His silence means that Job refuses any longer to recognize the forum of the friends. He takes his case to a higher court. From the very beginning Job had warned the friends that, with their speaking out against him, they stood in danger of committing a serious injustice (esp. 6:28-30). Now that has happened. They have leveled an accusation against him for which they have no proof. So now Job turns away from his friends in silence; he refuses to discourse any further with them. This act is the real conclusion to the disputation which began with the first speech of Eliphaz (chaps. 4-5). The same thing is obvious from the perspective of the friends; they can add nothing to the unrestrained, sweeping accusation in chap. 22. It is unlikely that they would now come prattling back with their earlier arguments. For their own part, they could not get beyond the fact that Job did not contest the accusation of Eliphaz at all.

But let us for a moment ignore the thesis that the dialogue section concludes with chap. 23. Whether that holds true or not, it has been shown in any case that the structure of the disputation between the friends and Job is sharp and clear, obviously segmented into three phases (the three cycles of discourse), and with a clearly recognizable internal progression. Added to that is the fact that the juxtaposition and interweaving of personal address and substantive discourse is recognizable and intelligible throughout all the speeches.

But all of this stops with chap. 24. Of course one can—and probably always will—attempt to construct some sort of conceptual connection here. It cannot be denied, however, that the composition recognizable up to this point ceases with chap. 24.[22] Not only on the basis of the questions which chaps. 24–27 themselves raise, but also on the basis of the determination of the form of the whole dialogue section, it is highly probable that these latter chapters have been only fragmentarily preserved.

With regard to the question of the original setting or the original context of these fragments, it must be presupposed that each of these pieces will initially have to be set in the context of its own proper genre—even though it is not always possible to isolate individual fragments and assign them with certainty to particular formal categories.

NOTES

1. Ludwig Köhler, "Justice in the Gate," postscript to *Hebrew Man,* trans. Peter R. Ackroyd (London: SCM, 1956), esp. pp. 159–60.

2. Köhler goes on to show in particular how these speeches are "a treasury for the legal formulas and advocates' phrases of the Hebrews" (ibid., p. 161); cf. Job 6:14–15a, 24; 8:2; 11:2–3; 12:2–3a; 15:2–3; 16:2–4.

3. Curt Kuhl, "Neuere Literarkritik des Buches Hiob," *Theologische Rundschau,* N.F. 21 (1953): 271–93.

4. Otto Eissfeldt, *The Old Testament: An Introduction,* trans. Peter R. Ackroyd (New York: Harper & Row, 1965), p. 468.

5. This applies only to the third speech of Eliphaz. From chap. 24 on the material is in fragmentary shape; insofar as it is composed of speeches by the friends, it contains only pieces of arguments without any element of personal address.

6. This criticism applies above all to Harry N. Torczyner, *Das Buch Hiob* (Vienna, 1920); Friedrich Baumgärtel, *Der Hiobdialog: Aufriss und Deutung,* Beiträge zur Wissenschaft vom Alten und Neuen Testament 61 (Stuttgart, 1933); and Paul Volz, *Das Buch Hiob,* Schriften des Alten Testaments 3/2 (Göttingen, 1911).

7. Here we see the use of *ykḥ* ("reprove") in the *hip'il,* against which Job defends himself in 6:25–26; on reproof of the "impudent" cf. Deut. 18:26 [*sic*]; Luke 18:9–14; Rom. 2:19–23. A separate investigation of this process throughout the whole Bible would be worthwhile.

8. Similarly in chap. 15 the reproof is connected with accusation: vv. 4–6 and 12–13. However, these accusations in chap. 15 are directed against the speech of Job in the course of the conversation. The accusations in chap.

22, on the other hand, precipitate a judgment upon the life that Job led prior to his being smitten by God.

9. Cf. the critical apparatus to Rudolf Kittel, ed., *Biblia Hebraica,* 3d ed. (Stuttgart, 1937). Georg Beer (*Der Text des Buches Hiob* [Marburg, 1897]), Bernhard Duhm (*Das Buch Hiob,* Kurzer Handkommentar zum Alten Testament 16 [Freiburg, 1897]), Carl Steuernagel (*Das Buch Hiob,* Heilige Schrift des Alten Testaments [Tübingen, ³1910], 2:293–356), and others also adopt this reading; John Gray ("The Book of Job in the Context of Near Eastern Literature," *Zeitschrift für die alttestamentliche Wissenschaft* 82 [1970]: 251–69) inclines toward it.

10. Cf. n. 2, above.

11. A stichos is apparently missing here, one which would have advanced the address in a scolding manner.

12. Cf. the critical apparatus to Kittel's *Biblia Hebraica,* which suggests the textual emendations here adopted.

13. Duhm correctly saw that, according to its sense, v. 2 is the consequence of v. 3. But one does not on that account need to transpose the verses. Duhm says: "Perhaps the turbulence of Zophar is supposed to find expression through this order of the sentences," or "this conceptual metathesis is a genuine sign of an agitated speech" (Duhm, *Das Buch Hiob,* p. 105).

14. The disputing precedes the accusation. Disputation still deals with the assembling of evidence and the determination of the state of affairs— the friends want to nail Job down to particular, incriminating statements ("you have said . . ." [11:4])—whereas the accusation is the conclusion drawn on the basis of the disputation.

15. Cf. n. 8, above.

16. The enumeration sounds stereotyped; it can hardly have been born of the moment. There are two possible origins of this enumeration: (1) It could come from the list of transgressions common in the social indictment *(Anklage)* of the prophets. Indeed, with only a few formal changes this enumeration could stand in any sort of prophetic indictment of the people of God! Just as the prophetic indictment provides grounds for the announcement of judgment, so here the accusation by Eliphaz is grounds for the punishment of God which has already befallen Job ("Therefore snares are round about you" [v. 10]). (2) However, there is still a more likely possibility. The consequence depicted in vv. 10–11 is not cast in terms of prophetic pronouncement of judgment. It is rather a motif drawn from the lament about enemies, in which the description of the matter is precisely this elaborate (cf. Ps. 140:5[6]; 141:9). As part of its theme of the "description of the transgressor," the lament about enemies not infrequently contains a depiction of the inhuman behavior of the transgressor (paralleling the other part of this theme, namely, the ungodliness of the transgressor). We can clearly assume that this is what we have here. However, the possibility is not to be rejected out of hand that sentences from the

prophetic indictment have subsequently worked their way into this part of the lament about enemies.

17. Baumgärtel, *Hiobdialog*, p. 144.

18. Similarly in the following:

> And they [the transgressors] say, "The Lord does not see;
> the God of Jacob does not perceive." (94:7)

> And they say, "How can God know?
> Is there knowledge in the Most High?" (73:11)

> The wicked despises God in his heart. . . . (10:3a)

> . . . There is no fear of God before his eyes. (36:1b[2b])

Cf. also Ps. 10:4, 11; 59:7[8]; 64:3[4].

19. It is peculiar but nonetheless deliberate that the emphasis in the speeches of the friends regularly falls on the first speech in the respective cycle of discourse, while in Job's speeches it just as clearly falls regularly on the last speech!

20. The last, ironic rejection of the "consolation" of the friends in 21:34 also has the character of finality about it.

21. And he *will* defend himself—that happens in chap. 31—but not before the court of the friends! With regard to Eliphaz, he needs only to refer to the contradiction between this friend's terrifying accusation (chap. 22) and his initial words (chap. 4:2–6).

22. Considerable difficulties begin to crop up already in chaps. 23–24.

3

The Laments of Job

The lament comprises by far the most prevalent formal element in
the Book of Job.[1] How extensively the speech of Job is dominated
by the lament can be demonstrated by this table:

First speech of Job:	6:4–20; 7:1–21
Second speech of Job:	9:17–31; 10:1–22
Third speech of Job:	(12:13–25); 13:20—14:22
Fourth speech of Job:	16:6—17:16
Fifth speech of Job:	19:7–20, 23, 27
Sixth speech of Job:	————

In addition there is the introductory lament of chap. 3 and the
concluding lament of chaps. 29–31.

The passages here enumerated are laments in a wider sense; included are elements of petition, wish, motivation, avowal of
trust—in other words, every sort of speech that gets addressed to
God. The lament in the strict sense, namely, that which corresponds
to the real lament portion in the psalms of lamentation, is in itself
segmented. In the case of the patent laments in chaps. 3 and 30, a
standard threefold articulation is immediately apparent: there is
lament directed to God (Lament I), self-lament (Lament II), and
lament about enemies (Lament III). In the dialogue section the relationship to one another of these three subcategories of the lament,
their distribution within the cycles of discourse, the development of
each of these subcategories, and the lack of one or another all con-
stitute essential parts of the dramatic composition. The recognition
of this threefold articulation of the lament grows out of study in
Psalms. It seems to me that this recognition makes the structure of

the speeches of Job more intelligible; the "dramatizing of the lament"[2] can really be perceived only when each of the three persons in the drama—God, Job, the friends—is heard as a particular voice being reflected through one of these subcategories of the lament throughout the whole dialogue section.

The Nature of the Lament and the Thesis of Baumgärtel

The words, sentences, and paragraphs in which Job speaks did not spring directly from the thought or imagination of a poet who may also have employed previously existing, traditional stylistic forms.[3] On the contrary, our poet stands within traditions which so determine his thought and shape his questions that he cannot express himself in other than already formed linguistic structures. We really cannot presuppose that the true point of origin of the Job-poem is the creative imagination or the spirit of a poet for whom everything sayable and thinkable is the material out of which he shapes something new—albeit thereby employing previously existing stylistic forms. Our poet's working method more nearly resembles that of the icon painter than that of a Renaissance artist. He dramatizes the lament by weaving together the basic motifs of lamentation, motifs which were already ancient in the time of our poet. To be sure, in his own time our poet's composition sounded forth a truly revolutionary call; however, its motifs are in the tones of the lament which lived in Israel's tradition and which, despite its wide variability, was familiar to all. For the poet of the Book of Job there is no such thing as thoughts about suffering, or reflective suffering; for him there is only real, experienced suffering. This real, experienced suffering is to be found not in abstract reflections but only in the reaction of a concrete human being to his own suffering—in a cry or in muffled silence or in the personal act of expressing this suffering, which means in a lament. What one happens to think about suffering is insignificant in the face of its reality. What one comes up with in brooding about the problem of suffering factually changes nothing. One has to admit that thoughts *about* suffering arise for the most part not down in the actual arena of suffering but up in the grandstand. Down in the arena there is real suffering, there may be lamenting and crying, perhaps with a summoning of all one's strength there is also silence, and God might even be praised in spite of everything—but there is no abstract reflecting about suffering. Down in the arena of suffering, life is not a "problem" but reality. And it is with the reality of suffering that the Book of Job deals; the book's setting is the arena not the grandstand. The lament is not a construct of thought; it is a living reality. It arises in a cry of pain. It is a cry that has become an utterance.[4] The Book of Job itself expresses this fact magnificently by having a cry stand at the beginning of the lament of Job. For what else is the cursing of the day of birth at the beginning of chap. 3 than just such a verbally transformed cry of pain? Several other times as well in the speeches of Job the lament almost comes out as a cry. At the end of his speaking, Job utters a summons to God (31:35-37) which, in juxtaposition, stands in close correspondence to the cry at the beginning (3:2-13).

The lament differs from the cry in being a word-event, and in the Old Testament that always means a personal event.[5] In the Old Testament a lament is something different from what we understand by that word today; there it always deals somehow with the lamenter himself, with God, and with certain other persons. The lament is a fixed form of speech having these three aspects or found with these three components; its history can be traced throughout the whole Old Testament.[6] The laments in the Book of Job also stand within this history. One must inquire about the place in the history of the lament in which our poet stands and what he has to declare at this point. In line with this inquiry, however, it is not very important to ask which sentences the poet of the Book of Job took over literally or thematically from the prior history of the lament and which sentences he himself composed. In any case, one could only rarely answer that question with full certainty, because only a portion of the laments voiced in ancient Israel have been transmitted to us in the psalms. Exegesis should rather start out from the fact that the lament is a living structure, a segmented whole; it has its fixed, regularly recurring parts. In any given case, the exegete must ask about the relationship of the parts to one another, about the predominance of one and the recession of another, about the development of a particular branch, about connections, fusions and new components, or about the rigidity of one particular part.

Only with constant attention to the living whole of the lament will the lamentation of Job in any one of his speeches be recognizable in its proper sense.

At this point I must come to terms with the work of Baumgärtel, who offers the most extreme counterproposals. With regard to a whole series of passages, Baumgärtel has laid out the parallels in the Psalter to the laments of Job in a more thorough and exhaustive fashion than has been previously done. I agree with Baumgärtel in the establishing of these parallels and in the assumption that there must be some connection between them. However, he goes on to conclude on the basis of the many concurrences that a lament properly so called, such as belongs to the psalms of lamentation, had no place in the original Job dialogue. All the places identified in Job as laments are to be expunged; such laments have no place in disputational speech. Baumgärtel is concerned to reconstruct out of the current format of the Book of Job a pure disputation speech. However, there are two reasons why this attempt cannot succeed: (1) *All* the speeches—both those of the friends and those of Job— consist of two parts. There is personal address (of the fellow disputant), and there is a substantive part, which in the case of the friends consists of theological arguments but in the case of Job consists almost entirely of laments (see above, p. 4). If one were to remove *all* the laments from the speeches of Job, only the framework would remain (cf. the table on p. 31). Because that would be impossible Baumgärtel does not actually cut out all the laments but rather only those parts of the laments which he thinks are too general and do not specifically relate to the case of Job. It has correctly been objected that Baumgärtel thus employs a subjective measuring stick and that any excision carried out completely along such lines could hardly win general assent. (2) On the other hand, the expunging of the laments yields a Job-dialogue which cannot possibly have the character ascribed to it on the last page of Baumgärtel's book (see n. 4). Consider, for example, his exegesis of the first speech of Job: "On the whole no objection can be raised against the authenticity of chap. 6. Here there is a well-constructed composition easily understandable on its own terms." He continues:

Chapter 7 does not stand in any organic connection with its preceding chapter. . . . Up to this point the friends are the ones being addressed; now there suddenly appears a "you" referring to God (vv.

7, 8, 14, etc.). Likewise the tenor is suddenly quite different. Up to this point the zealous and defiant Job. . . . Now an elegaic and sad lament which is distinct from the kind of lamenting found up to this point. Job laments about his suffering, but now he connects it . . . with the suffering of mankind in general. . . . That has to appear exceptionally strange in relation to the prior context.

Baumgärtel elaborates upon this point and comes to this conclusion:

> Therefore these statements of chap. 7 stand in total opposition to those of chap. 6. . . . Chapter 7 is a fully independent poem that has no necessary relationship to Job whatsoever. It is a psalmlike song of a miserable leper, as we find, for example, in Psalm 88. Given its manifold conceptual contacts with the Book of Job, Psalm 88 could just as easily fit into the context of this book as does our psalm in chap. 7. There is no fundamental difference here at all. Chapter 7 is . . . an independent, self-standing song of a sufferer who believes that his suffering is too severe a punishment for his sins (pp. 26–28).

The question at once arises whether or not this is precisely Job's situation. Furthermore, if in his song this sufferer unites his suffering with the suffering of mankind in general, why should not the same thing be possible with Job? However, these questions do not yet touch the core of the matter. In the first place, Baumgärtel's observations, especially regarding the comparison with Psalm 88, are certainly correct and are essential for the understanding of the Job-speeches. However, these observations permit a different conclusion. Baumgärtel's conclusion, namely, that the essential similarity of chap. 7 to Psalm 88 shows this chapter to be a foreign body in the Job-dialogue, probably has very close similarities to our way of thinking. However, this conclusion can be drawn with certainty only if chap. 6 now employs a sort of language fundamentally different from the psalms, which is to say, only if the difference between the passages left intact and those stricken from the Book of Job can be demonstrated on form-critical or stylistic grounds. Kuhl is right in objecting that this step is not really carried out by Baumgärtel: "Only one thing . . . is missing in this whole theory: a stylistic comparison between the passages held to be authentic and those judged secondary."[7] But in fact such a comparison between chap. 6 and chap. 7 yields no real distinction, as will now be demonstrated.

Psalm 88, which Baumgärtel likens to chap. 7, itself refutes his most important argument for the removal of chap. 7. Baumgärtel finds an abrupt and unintelligible change from chap. 6 to chap. 7; he understands chap. 7 to be "an elegaic and sad lament, distinct from the sort of lamenting found up to this point." However, just such a change is also found in Psalm 88. Verses 4–6 are comprised of self-lament; in v. 7 second-person lament—directed to God—immediately starts up and is then continued in vv. 15–19 (Psalm 88 is in a fragmented state; v. 19 cannot possibly have been the original conclusion of the psalm). What Baumgärtel has correctly observed here is the transition from one component of the lament to another. This transition from self-lament to lament directed to God (or vice versa) occurs regularly in the psalms of lamentation, as it does in the Book of Job; it grows out of the very structure of the lament. Chapter 7 is readily understandable once it is recognized that the lament is a segmented whole in which one particular component never occurs without at least one of the other two. Obviously this transition from one component of the lament to another shows up much more clearly in the Book of Job than in the psalms; a particular component of the lament within the psalms of lamentation rarely consists of more than four verses, whereas these components in the Book of Job are considerably more extensive.

Another argument of Baumgärtel for the removal of chap. 7 is the expansion from the suffering of Job to the suffering of mankind in general. Here as well one finds obvious parallels in the psalms of lamentation. Psalm 39 is the lament of an individual suffering from a specific malady who turns to God in supplication. The specificity is obvious in vv. 2–3[3–4] and especially in v. 10[11]:

> Remove from me your plague;
>> under the "weight" of your hand I waste away.

Nevertheless the psalm is dominated not by the particular suffering of the supplicant but rather by the general fate of mankind:

> You chastise a man with punishment for his guilt;
>> his grandeur you allow to vanish like fodder for a moth,
>> surely every man is a mere breath! (v. 11[12b])

The same motif is further developed in vv. 4–6[5–7]. The psalm also shows obvious linguistic connections with the Book of Job;[8] the lament directed to God in this psalm (vv. 12–13[13–14]) likewise sounds familiar. It is therefore apparent that expanding the lament of a sufferer to include reference to the common fate of mankind can occur together with lament directed to God within a psalm of lamentation of only thirteen verses. If this is so, then the argument for the removal of chap. 7 cannot be maintained.

It remains to be asked whether in fact only chap. 7—and not also chap. 6 —resembles the psalms of lamentation. Chapter 6 contains a great deal of disputational speech in particular and thereby corresponds to the criterion Baumgärtel applies. However, insofar as this disputational speech contains within itself parts of the lament, it can be shown with certainty that these parts speak the language of the psalms of lamentation and reflect their particular motifs.[9] That only the parts of the Job-laments excised by Baumgärtel have obvious parallels in the psalms of lamentation does not prove to be true.[10]

The Lament of Job at the Beginning: Chapter 3

The structure of the third chapter is simple and clear. The parts are delimited by the "why" questions in v. 11 and v. 20. The part beginning in 3:11 is introduced by the mournful question "Why did I . . . ?" and the part beginning in 3:20 by "Why is . . . ?" Both these components of the lament, namely, the self-lament (or self-complaint) in vv. 11–19 and the lament directed to God in vv. 20–23, are thus immediately apparent. Usually the lament directed to God is cast in the second person (you = God), but here this is intentionally not done; only gradually does it break through to its full sharpness, being here at the outset very indirectly worded. Verses 24–26 once again contain self-lament, more precisely, a particular element of this sort of lament, namely, a description of mourning.[11] In vv. 3–9, in place of the customary third component of the lament (the lament about enemies), stands Job's cursing of his day of birth (the day of birth is a substitute for the enemy). Verses 3–9 comprise a widely expanded malediction, while v. 10 is its motivation clause.[12] This first part[13] determines the whole chapter in such a way that this chapter strikes one as being especially unified and complete. The self-lament dominates in this chapter; the cursing of the day of birth substantively belongs to this component as well (it very closely resembles a self-complaint), although formally it corresponds to the third component of the lament (the lament about enemies). The self-lament here at the beginning follows not the traditional form as derived from the psalms of lamentation but rather the primordial form of the self-lament, whose combination with the cursing of the day of birth was already established.[14] It is noteworthy that Job's lament starts out with this untamed form of the lament, rooted in the early times.[15] The basic components of the chapter are thus the cursing of the day of birth (with motivation clause—v. 3 and v. 10—formally corresponding to the lament about enemies), the self-lament (v. 11, whose older and purer form appears in Jer. 20:18), and the lament directed to God (v. 23). The chapter's conclusion (vv. 24–26) is formed by the self-lament along traditional lines.

The Lament of Job at the End: Chapters 29–31

In this long concluding speech of Job, lament in the true sense of the word is found only in chap. 30. It is encompassed by the asseveration of innocence, or oath of clearance (chap. 31), and by Job's retrospection upon his earlier good fortune (chap. 29). The relation of chap. 31 to the lament is obvious. The asseveration of innocence is a fixed, frequently encountered compositional element of the individual lament psalm.[16] It is one of the various sorts of inducements meant to prompt God's intervention. An asseveration of innocence fulfilling this function is to be found in the lament in chap. 30 itself, at v. 35. This verse could just as well stand in chap. 31, and in fact it corresponds substantively to 31:29–32. We know of examples from the Psalter where this motif is the main part of the psalm or has even developed into an independent psalm.[17] Job 31 is to be understood in the same way. The fact that just this motif from the lament becomes the final, emphatic utterance of Job is based on the whole of the Job-drama. It serves as the rejoinder to the accusation in the final speech of Eliphaz, which is itself the culmination of all the speeches of the friends. However, this rejoinder is no longer directed to the friends; Job no longer recognizes in his friends a court of justice. He instead voices his rebuttal, in the form of a solemn self-cursing, in the presence of God, following a custom certainly originating in the Israelite cultus. After the introductory vv. 1-4,[18] this long chapter consists essentially of manifold variations on ever the same form of speech, with the variations referring to the differing spheres of human existence. The same phenomenon occurs in Ps. 7:3-5[4-6].[19]

The motivation clauses in the individual lament psalms always appear in conjunction with the element of petition.[20] The same is true here in 31:35-37. To be sure, v. 35 is not a petition but a wish. However, that accords with the usual state of affairs in such poems, in which direct petition yields primacy of place to indirect wish. The verbs in this wish are elsewhere found in pure petitions.[21] Following the wish is a summoning of God, cast completely in legal terminology. Job's answers to the speeches of the friends have already prepared the way for such language. In these concluding verses (31:35-37), lament and demand for a legal hearing, the two fundamental proceedings which determine the speeches of Job, converge once more in a final climax. Here at the end Job stands before God as simultaneously a supplicant and an initiator of a legal proceeding. That is the impossible but nonetheless actual "standpoint" of Job; he stands there and awaits God's answer.

Chapter 29 resembles chap. 31 in that it contains a single, widely expanded theme. However, this theme is not immediately recognizable as an expansion upon one of the components of the individual lament psalm. The whole chapter is a retrospective look at Job's earlier good fortune, and, to be sure, it has the form of an expanded wish: "Oh, that I were as in the months of old, when . . ." (vv. 2-5). This is a form of speech immediately understandable in the light of Job's situation; no demonstration of the genre's origin is called for. Yet for all that, it would be surprising if there were no prehistory here, since most of the compositional elements in the Book of Job do point back to earlier forms of speech. Now admittedly there is no such element as a "retrospective look at God's earlier salvific activity" in the individual lament psalms (there is a hint of such in Ps. 143:5). However, this element does appear in the communal lament psalms; Ps. 80 offers a particularly good example of it.[22] The import of this motif is the setting out of the contrast between God's earlier and his present activity.[23] It is probable that this same motif underlies Job 29. This chapter from Job differs, however, in that the lamenting consists not only in a review of *God's* earlier salvific activity but also—indeed especially—in a more general review of the earlier state of being. In the structure of the chapter, therefore, the three subjects of the lament are reflected: God (vv. 2-4), self (vv. 4a-5b, 12-20), and the others (vv. 7-11, 21-25).[24] Since in chap. 29 the three components of the lament stand in obvious contrast, it is certainly intentional that the lament in chap. 30 begins with the same component with which chap. 29 ends, namely, that of "the others."

As for chap. 30, this speech about the present, which stands in such terrifying contrast to the felicitous past, can only be lament. It is obviously a lament developed in the threefold manner, starting out with accusation against the enemies (vv. 1-15). Next comes the element of self-lamentation (vv. 16-19, 24-31); set within this self-lamentation is the accusation against God (vv. 20-23). Verses 1-15 have an obvious caesura after v. 8; v. 9a corresponds formally to v. 1a. While vv. 1-8 describe the nature of those who scorn Job, vv. 9-15 shift the perspective and look at the actions of Job's mockers. This corresponds to the juxtaposition of the two groups of statements concerning enemies as found in the individual lament psalms: the actions of the enemies—the nature of the enemies.[25] The actions of the enemies bemoaned about to God almost always consist in an attack upon the lamenter. Three clusters of images are used to describe the attack: (1) the enemies set nets or traps, (2) the enemies are wild beasts who fall upon the lamenter, and (3) the enemies are attacking warriors.[26] The third cluster of images dominates in Job 30:9-15; vv. 12-14 develop only this one metaphor.[27] This matter of the enemies assailing the lamenter is not understandable solely in the light of Job's situation.[28] The subject of vv. 12-14 corresponds neither to the subject of vv. 2-8 nor to that of 29:7-10, and in this sense it is true that the piece "hangs in the air."[29] But one can understand this chapter only if one sees behind it the structure of the individual lament psalm. Job's lament draws its very life from the themes of the individual lament psalm. Being assailed by enemies is a fixed motif of the lament about enemies, and the particularities in the description should not and cannot directly be related to Job's own situation. The poet of the Book of Job has Job voice his lament in the ways available to him out of the traditions of his day. Job laments as anyone would have lamented in any conceivable situation.[30] The artistry of the poet lies precisely in the fact that he incorporated the ancient lament themes into his poem in such a way that his hearers had to sense on their own and discover for themselves the point of comparison between the traditional lament motif and the particularity of this precise moment in the Job-drama. In this case it is simple: the element of being assailed by enemies is, for Job, equivalent to that which the friends—now turned to enemies—had sought throughout the whole disputation speech. They are the enemies who earlier had highly esteemed Job but now, while not really scorning him, nevertheless reckon him among the transgressors.

The self-lament begins at v. 16; the "and now" (*wə'attāh*) marks the new starting point. Verse 16 closely resembles v. 27; the self-lament is continued in vv. 27–31. We had already found in chap. 3 that the accusation against God was encompassed by the self-lament; the same holds true here. Yet in chap. 30 the transition from self-lament to accusation against God is difficult to recognize because the text is disrupted. Probably vv. 18–23 are to be understood as accusation against God;[31] they correspond to the accusation against God in chap. 3 (vv. 20–23). There the initial, intimated accusation starts out, "Why is light given to him that is in misery, and life to the bitter in soul?" (3:20a). Here the final accusation against God concludes with "Yea, I know that thou wilt bring me to death" (30:23a). This knowledge is grounded in the fact that Job has cried to God but God has not answered him (v. 20). When God is silent, that means death.[32] The same lament occurs already in 19:7; looking backward (12:4) and forward (13:22; 14:15), Job knows that for him everything depends upon God's answer. However, the God who no longer answers has become for Job a demon: "You have turned into a ruthless tyrant for me" (v. 21).[33] Verse 22 depicts the activity of this God who has become a demon: God seizes Job and gives him up to the forces of the high places, to the storm and the raging of the elements. According to vv. 18–19, God seizes Job, constrains him, and hurls him down into the dirt and the ashes.[34] This God who has become a demon can only will Job's death (v. 23). However, even this accusation against God which stands on the very brink of blasphemy, of which one assumes that it can be spoken *only* here, has its obvious parallels in the Psalter.[35]

Verses 24-26 form a transition between the accusation against God concluded in v. 23 and the self-lament resumed in v. 27.[36]

As for vv. 27-31, this last part of the concluding lament of Job clearly reminds one of the initial lament of Job in 3:24-26. All the clauses of this self-lament once again take up traditional lament themes;[37] no clause in 30:27-31 is totally without its corresponding parallel. The verses essentially contain a description of mourning and pain.[38]

Thus the lament of Job is concluded. Yet in the psalms of lamentation the lament proper is never the whole; it is always only one part. The situation is no different in the Book of Job even though here the theme of lamentation widely dominates. All the other components characteristic of a psalm of lamentation are also to be found in the Book of Job. In a psalm of lamentation petition usually follows the lament, the petition often being conjoined with motivation clauses. In the place of the motivation clause, here in the Book of Job we find the whole of chap. 31 (see above, pp. 38-39); then there follows in the place of the petition the wish in 31:35-37 (see above, p. 39). The structure of the psalm of lamentation is recognizable in its totality despite considerable poetic alteration.[39]

The Laments of Job within the Disputation Speeches

The threefold compositional structure of the laments, worked out as it was for chaps. 3 and 30, likewise determines the laments of Job within the disputational discourse. Now one must keep in mind that, with the laments, we are dealing with the constant elements in the speeches of Job; the lament-themes remain essentially the same, with variations serving only to emphasize the arrangement and the selection of themes. However, the themes of the lament are *everywhere* the themes traditional in Israel. They are the same themes we meet in the psalms of lamentation; not a single theme from Job is totally unparalleled in the psalms transmitted to us. To be sure, the formulations often deviate widely, and considerable dissimilarity arises from the fact that the development of the lament-themes is consistently more extensive in the Book of Job than it is in the psalms of lamentation; the lament has become true poetry in the Book of Job. Nevertheless, the fact remains that the laments of Job are essentially laments which a supplicant might also have voiced in Psalms.

This is not the place for a conclusive demonstration of this.[40] We can only trace with broad strokes how the themes of the lament in the speeches of Job fit together into a surprisingly clear, well-demarcated whole. In order to show this it is necessary to take a look first at the components of the lament in isolation.

The Lament about Enemies

The third component of the lament, the lament about enemies, hardly appears in the laments of Job in the dialogue section. It occurs clearly only in the first and fifth speeches, and in both these places it is not lament about enemies in the true sense of the word. On the contrary, both passages (6:13-20 and 19:13-19) present variations on the theme. It is easy to explain why the lament about enemies in the true sense—that is, the indictment before God of the enemies oppressing the supplicant—is missing in the speeches of Job in the dialogue section. Here altercation with the friends who become Job's enemies has intruded into the place of the true lament about enemies. This transition from lament about enemies to altercation is clearly depicted in the first speech of Job in the way in which vv. 21-27 follow vv. 13-20 of chap. 6. In 6:13-20 we find a variation on the lament about enemies: in the place of the enemies there appear the friends, relatives, confidants, and neighbors of the lamenter insofar as they have turned against the lamenter or even merely turned away from him. One frequently encounters this variation on the lament about enemies in the individual lament psalms.[41] An expansion of this motif occurs when the lamenter speaks of his former friendship, intimacy, or even love to those who now stand against him.[42] All these passages say that the friends of the lamenter have become his enemies. This motif from Psalms has echoes in the Book of Job. The image of the "treacherous torrent-bed" in 6:15-20 is a gripping variation on this general theme; the verses here singularly develop this one image. The same image occurs in one of the laments of Jeremiah, in an accusation against

God: "You have become to me like a deceitful brook, like water upon which one cannot rely" (Jer. 15:18). However, it is not to be assumed that this image is original to Jeremiah's accusation against God; certainly a lament about a friend who has proven untrue would have employed this image already before Jeremiah. Thus our passage in Job reflects the original context of this particular image, which was then employed with great audacity by Jeremiah in reference to God.

Verse 21 goes on to address the friends directly: "Such you have now become to me." This move completes the transition to disputation speech from indictment of the friends who have turned into enemies. The transition is made cautiously in the first speech of Job in the dialogue section; from here on in the whole dialogue section disputation speech appears in place of lament about enemies. Only in the concluding lament of Job, in 30:1-15, does the lament about enemies once again appear, namely, after it is conclusively determined that Job's friends have indeed become his enemies. Thus with considerable artistry the poet has quite imperceptibly inserted the lament form of speech—the form which determines the speeches of Job—into the disputational discourse. The disputation speech of Job thus secondarily occupies the place of one of the components of the lament, namely, the lament about enemies.

The other variation on the lament about enemies is to be found in Job 19:13-19, which is the only other segment of a lament about enemies to be found in the dialogue section. The passage starts out in much the same way as the one in 6:13-20:

> My brethren are treacherous . . . (6:15)
> My brethren have withdrawn from me . . . (19:13)

The two passages have a common subject, but they differ in their predicates. While the lament in 6:15-20 consists of a single sentence which is then illustrated by means of the image, in this lament a whole series of events is unfolded. There the focus is upon an act: the friends have failed. Here the focus is upon a state, which has been brought about through many acts. All the groups of people in the circle around the lamenter contribute to this state. Job laments that all the people in his personal milieu have turned away from him!

Once again Psalms shows that we are here dealing with another variation on the lament about enemies. A precise parallel, standing in conjunction with the lament about enemies which follows it, is to be found in Ps. 38:11[12]:[43]

My friends and companions stand aloof . . .
and my kinsmen stand afar off.

And so, in both passages within the dialogue section of Job where lament is directed against others, the two variations on the lament about enemies which we know from Psalms show up. Both these variations, namely, the lament about the friends upon whom one can no longer rely and the lament about family and friends who turn away from one, fit right in with Job's situation. The lament about enemies in the strict sense of the word, however, does not really apply to Job's situation. Such a lament about enemies can come up only after the conclusion of the dialogue section, where it has been proven to Job that his friends have now finally become his enemies.

On the other hand, in the course of the Job-drama there emerges the shocking transformation by which God himself becomes an enemy to Job. This is shown most clearly in 16:9-14 and 19:7-12, which are accusations against God in the form and with the traditional images and vocabularies of the lament about enemies. Substantively these passages belong in the context of accusation against God, and this is how they are spoken. To anticipate a bit with a formal observation, note that these accusations against God in the form of a lament about enemies occur only in the fourth and fifth speeches of Job, which is to say, in the second cycle of discourse. Here also the second cycle of discourse is obviously contrasted with the first. On top of that, only in these two speeches do we find an avowal of trust. In other words, precisely where Job utters the sharpest and most dangerous words against God he also speaks the words which nevertheless most clearly show him holding fast to God. Once again we see the astoundingly clear and powerful architectonic of the book. In these two speeches of the second cycle of discourse the two most extreme points of tension occur in such close proximity that the alert hearer *must* sense the oscillation of the tension in the Job-drama between these poles of accusation and avowal of trust. Only with an ear attuned to this polarity can one properly hear the Book of Job.[44] Additional, openly expressed laments about enemies do not occur in the dialogue section.[45]

The Self-lament

The self-lament in the first speech of Job (chaps. 6-7) in the dialogue section takes up considerable room. Although 6:1-12 is an utterance directed to the friends, the self-lament actually dominates it. Here Job's suffering is not yet concretely described; the lament primarily bemoans the reality of his suffering as such. The three sections of this self-lament together form an enclosed unity; each individual section deals with the facticity, the undeniable reality of Job's suffering. Verses 2-3a deal with the severity of Job's suffering, vv. 5-7 with the reality of his suffering (through comparison with the wailing of beasts), vv. 11-12 with the unbearableness of his suffering. Not until 7:3-5 does the particular, concrete nature of Job's suffering find expression. The clause in 7:3 corresponds to the "introductory lament" in the psalms of lamentation—that is, those clauses at the beginning of a whole set of psalms of lamentation, clauses which are affixed to the introductory petition to serve as a motivation clause (usually introduced by the particle *kî*).[46] Generalized designations for suffering find their proper place in these introductory laments. Often these introductory laments are intensified by statements referring to temporal duration, such as "For all the day long I have been stricken, and chastened every morning" (Ps. 73:14).[47] Job 7:4 is like this; Job is tormented without interruption. Verse 4 therefore belongs immediately after v. 3 as an intensifying expansion.[48] The lament about disease in v. 5 follows on this expanded introductory lament (cf. Ps. 69:29[30]); this verse is Job's first concrete lament in the dialogue section. It is noteworthy that laments about disease occur only rarely in the Book of Job. To be sure, there is a whole series of allusions to Job's particular disease. Explicit laments about disease, however, laments which describe the symptoms of some physical ailment, actually occur only here in 7:5 and in the concluding lament at 30:17 and 30:30. Since in both places the lament about disease is associated with the introductory lament, one suspects here the presence of a fixed form. Apparently we see here the sort of beginning typical of

one group of laments in which isolated lament themes get drawn
into a larger whole by the presence of a very brief lament about
disease. In both chap. 7 and chap. 30 the lament about disease
obviously stands in an emphatic position, but both times the lament
encompasses only one verse (this happens twice in chap. 30). It is
noteworthy that chap. 3 contains no specific lament about disease.[49] The noticeable barrenness and shortness of the element of
lament about disease in the Book of Job is certainly grounded in
Israelite tradition; detailed description of disease never occurs in
Psalms. In the Babylonian psalms of lamentation, on the other
hand, a lament about disease occasionally exhibits considerable
expansion.[50] We do not know the grounds for Israel's reluctance to
describe diseases extensively before God.

The passage just discussed (7:3–5) belongs to a larger section encompassing 7:1–10, the whole of which is a self-lament. After the
lament about disease in v. 5, Job goes on in vv. 6–10 to bemoan the
hopelessness and the inescapable finitude of his existence. This
theme was even more expansively generalized upon in vv. 1–2.
Within the context of a whole section, however, the specialized self-
lament in vv. 3–5 forms the midpoint, and only from this central
core are vv. 1–2 and 6–10 to be understood. In a reflective mood,
Job places his unique, solitary suffering into the broad perspective
of the futility of human existence in general. This is nothing different from what happens in chap. 3, only there it is much more obvious that the starting point is the narrow circle of Job's own suffering, the diameter of which is then so widened as to reach the
outer circle of human suffering in general. Whenever one feels op-
pressed by the realization of one's own helplessness, one naturally
reaches out to the boundaries beyond one's own oppression. This
tendency toward generalization is an intrinsic aspect of lamentation. Everyone who has fallen under the burden of severe difficulty
knows the inclination to generalize on the basis of his particular
distress. This process of generalization has existential rather than
literary causes. Therefore, in these passages in which self-lament is
expanded to lament about the common lot of mankind, we are by
no means justified in seeing yet another literary genre, namely, wisdom speech. Admittedly this reflective way of expanding a self-
lament has its affinities to wisdom speech. However, the origin of

this sort of speech undoubtedly lies in the self-lament, as chap. 3 especially shows. The same tendency to reflective expansion is recognizable in a number of psalms of lamentation.[51]

The references to human finitude in all these passages in the individual lament psalms are meant to work some sort of effect upon God. In the passages just referred to above, one can see how this motif gets elaborated upon, how it breaks off from the element of petition to which it innately belongs and becomes an independent element. There can be no doubt that in Job 7:1-10 we are dealing with precisely this sort of motif; therefore Job's speech about the hopelessness of human existence was originally and properly an utterance directed to God, which only gradually became a reflective speech about the nature of human existence in general. The original character of the references to the transitoriness of human life is still very clearly recognizable in 7:6-10; in v. 7 the motif gets carried over into direct petition of God: "Remember that my life is a breath" (cf. 7:16).

This line of thought is carried out even further in the second speech of Job. The self-lament proper, as we encountered it in 6:1-12 and 7:3-5, moves completely to the background in chaps. 9-10. The lament about human finitude, which already in chap. 7 resounded more loudly than the self-lament proper and which formed the connecting link to the accusation against God,[52] appears alone in chaps. 9-10, in the place of self-lament, and is here even more tightly woven in with the accusation against God. The connection shows up in 9:25-31, a lament about the transitoriness of human existence ("My days are swifter than a runner. . ."); note how vv. 27-28 bring in the motif of continual suffering, the same motif as in 7:4 and 3:26. The second speech concludes with this theme of transitoriness (10:18-22), whereby vv. 20-22 take up the theme of chap. 7 while vv. 18-19 point back to chap. 3, with the difference being that the lament from chap. 3 ("Why have I been born?") is here in chap. 10 taken up into the accusation against God ("Why didst thou bring me forth from the womb?"). Once more the same train of thought shows up: the self-lament which dominates at the beginning is progressively absorbed into accusation against God.[53]

Self-lament in the strict sense of the word no longer occurs in the third speech of Job (chaps. 12-14). Significantly, the self-lament of chap. 3 once again resonates at the end of chap. 10 (vv. 18–19, see above). *This* self-lament has here come to an end; the circle closes at this point. After this point in the third speech only the expansion of the self-lament, namely, the bemoaning of human finitude, is carried on. This occurs in 14:1–15; the section has two parts: vv. 1–6 and vv. 7–15. Both parts end in a petition or a wish: v. 6 and vv. 13–15. We found the same in chap. 7. Serving as it does primarily to stimulate action, this expansion is closely allied with the element of petition; it is a bridge from lament to petition. The two aspects of the lament about human transitoriness appear clearly in both parts: in 14:1–5 the concern is primarily with the fact of human finitude, or the exterior aspect of transitoriness; in 14:7–12 the concern is more with the interior side, the sense of hopelessness that accompanies finite being. Both aspects were already alluded to in the two stichoi in 7:6. How deliberately these two aspects have been further developed is shown in the way the second speech stresses the *exterior* aspect of finitude (10:8b, 9b), while the third speech takes up the *interior* aspect of finitude into the accusation against God (14:19b). As a rule the exterior aspect of human finitude is emphasized in the second speech, while its interior aspect is stressed in the third speech.[54]

The fourth speech of Job (chaps. 16–17) ends in a self-lament in which the interior and exterior aspects of human finitude are closely intertwined.[55] Furthermore, Job here utters as his personal lament a general lament about the fate of mankind. With this the circle of lamentation about the fate of mankind, which in chap. 7 had separated itself from personal lamentation, closes and is again absorbed by personal lamentation. At the same time this fourth speech displays yet another motif of the self-lament, namely, the description of lamenting. We had previously encountered this motif only in the introductory lament in chap. 3, at v. 24.[56] Job 17:1 is the transition from description of lamenting to lament about human finitude. Job 17:4–10 has undoubtedly been dislodged from its original context and now intrudes. Job 17:6–8, which unfortunately is also textually uncertain, belongs to the self-lament in chaps. 16–17 and even introduces a new motif. After Job has rejected the "miserable comfort" of his friends in vv. 2–5, he says in vv. 6–8 that his lament is pointless. It makes no difference whether he speaks or not (v. 6); insofar as he bemoans his suffering, even this is held up as testimony against him (v. 8). His lament succeeds only in indirectly confirming his guilt—or at least this is what the friends maintain.

With this the element of self-lament, which totally dominated at the beginning of the speech of Job and then ever so gradually retreated, is finally shattered. It has become pointless. Thus with this fourth speech the self-lament in the dialogue section ceases.[57] Only in the concluding lament in chap. 30 do we once again find self-lament; the concluding section of the final lament of Job is self-lament (30:24–31) just as the initial lament of Job was essentially self-lament. In this final section there once again come together a whole array of motifs. It would hardly be possible to find one train of thought here. The self-lament of Job, with which chap. 3 had so boldly started out and which was then gradually muted and transformed into general lamentation about the transitoriness of human existence, resounds in heavy monotone one last time at the very end.

The Accusation against God

The shift away from self-lament toward accusation against God is recognizable already in the introductory lament of Job in chap. 3; it is intimated in the cursing of the day of birth at the very outset. The curse is directed against the one who gave life to Job. Here at the beginning the focus is upon the day of birth, but behind the scene stands God, as 3:20 likewise suggests. Both in the cry at the beginning of chap. 3 and also in vv. 20–23 accusation against God is already on the horizon. The whole section is cast in the third person. Only v. 23 contains a real accusation against God: "God has obstructed my way." Through its indirect object, the interrogative of v. 20 implies a self-lament; vv. 21–22 elaborate upon the indirect object of v. 20. In terms of its form, this elaboration includes also v. 23. The whole section is therefore basically just an expansion upon the interrogative of v. 20, which itself is closely tied in with the self-lament which dominates the chapter.

The First Speech of Job, Chapters 6–7

Job subtantiates his apology in 6:2–3 with an indirect accusation against God in v. 4: "For the arrows of the Almighty are in me, my spirit drinks their poison, the terrors of God 'disquiet' me." The theme taken up here is developed at the end of this speech, in 7:11–21. This final section is newly introduced (v. 11), as though the lament were now beginning in earnest. What comes to the fore is that the accusation against God beginning here is really a lament. Alternately expressed, it is the kernel of the lament, just as the accusation against God in v. 4 is the real basis for the apology of Job in vv. 2–3.

The section 7:12–21 has an obvious caesura after v. 16; vv. 12–16 are essentially declarative statements, while vv. 17–21 are almost all questions. Here in the first continuous passage of accusation against God, we meet with both the two chief forms of accusation against God: declarative statement and interrogative query.[58]

With regard to the declarations in vv. 12–16, the real accusation comes in v. 12: God sets a guard over Job as over the sea or the dragon of chaos. This ties in directly with 6:4; in 6:4 the thought is of martial combat, while in 7:12 it is of the struggle against chaos. A motif common to praise of God stands behind the imagery here.[59] God is praised as the one who has conquered the powers of chaos and holds them in bounds.[60] Verses 13–14 correspond to 6:4c;[61] the theme of the terror of God is developed in such a way that a motif from the self-lament, namely, the incessant nature of suffering, is taken up into the accusation against God.

As for vv. 17–21, the clauses in vv. 17–18 taken together raise the question "Why?" as do vv. 20–21a; v. 19 asks the question "How long?" These two lamenting questions characteristically occur together in accusations against God in the psalms of lamentation.[62]

The Second Speech of Job, Chapters 9–10

The accusation against God dominates in this speech. It begins right away in the agreeing with Bildad that, indeed, a human being cannot be just before God (9:2–3). Job substantiates this through his praise of the majesty of God (9:4–13) and then takes up once more the agreement at the beginning (9:14–16), intensifying it even more: over against God mankind forever remains absolutely subjected, with no alternative but to turn to God in supplication. Herein lies already the transition to accusation against God, which now (9:17–23) breaks through with incisive sharpness. In chaps.

6-7 the accusation against God referred to God as the enemy of Job, as the hostile warrior and as the one who sets the boundaries of chaos. Job 9:17 connects up with this; God is like a howling tempest that lays hold of a person and snatches him away. Motifs of the self-lament are taken up in this accusation, such as pain (v. 17b), bitterness (v. 18b), and the incessant nature of it all (v. 18a). Then there follows once again a true accusation: God allows might to overrule right (vv. 19-20). In the face of this might Job cries out in his asseveration of innocence (vv. 21-22) and then drives his accusation against God to its climax: God is unjust (vv. 22b and 24b). Verse 23 takes up the imagery of the introductory v. 17a in somewhat altered fashion and so rounds off this section (vv. 17-23) into a terrifying picture of a raging God who slashes at those around him with a whip and laughs at the despairing of the innocent. In the self-lament which follows (9:25—10:1a), this frightful accusation against God continues to resound. In the presence of the angry God, it is a matter of indifference whether one is guilty or innocent (vv. 28b and 30-31).[63] While the accusations against God in chap. 9 are declarative statements, in chap. 10 the interrogative form of accusation dominates, starting right in with 10:2.[64] Verse 3 carries this interrogative query a step further. In both these verses, Job inquires of God as the lord of history ("Why do you contend against me?"[65]) and as the creator ("Why do you scorn the work of your hands?"). The contradiction implied by these questions is broadly developed in 10:8-17.[66] Verse 8 takes up the accusation of v. 3, with vv. 9-12 expanding upon v. 8a and vv. 13-17 expanding upon v. 8b. It is clear that v. 8, taken in isolation, presents a motif of praise of God—praise of the creator, specifically the creator of mankind. Psalm 139:13-16 offers a remote parallel. Here the full artistry of the poet of Job comes to light. Praise of the creator, which Job lifted at the beginning of his answer to Bildad (9:4-13), is again taken up here at the end of the same speech. At the outset the praise was of the creator of all creatures; here it is of the one who has created Job himself. Both times this praise of the creator is only a step removed from accusation; thereby the accusation of chap. 9 is clearly intensified as one moves on into chap. 10. The imagery of God as an enemy builds up in the concluding vv. 16-17. God is compared to a devouring beast (v. 16), an opponent in a lawsuit (v. 17a), and a leader of a hostile army (v. 17b). With v. 18 the accusation returns once again to the interrogative format of vv. 3–7, and with vv. 18–19 the lament of Job goes back once more to its starting point—to Job's question about the meaning of his existence ("Why was I born?"). This latter question has by now become an accusation against God ("Why didst *thou* bring me forth from the womb?"). Obviously a cycle comes to a close here.

The Third Speech of Job, Chapters 12–14

The accusation against God in chaps. 9–10 strikes one as a high point that is hard to surpass.[67] The accusation against God only intimated in chap. 3 is so intensified through chaps. 6–7 and on into this zenith in chaps. 9–10 that one has to ask how the continuance of this theme in chaps. 12–14 is to be understood.

In 13:1ff. Job turns totally away from his friends and thereby turns exclusively toward God (13:3, 14–16). The utterance now directed to God in 13:23–27, after extensive and laborious introduction, is no longer the same sort of utterance as the accusations against God right up to the previous speech. In 13:17–19 the formal legal dispute with God is introduced, obviously employing the official juristic speech patterns of the day.[68] In 13:23–27 Job makes a preliminary inquiry, asking God to make known the legal basis for his treatment of Job. Two specific forms of speech fall together here; the inquiry about the legal basis, which is part of a legal proceeding,[69] coincides with the interrogative query of the accusation against God as one component of the lament. The quite extensive introductory section of this passage (13:24–27) again breaks through to the primitive interrogative character of the queries and dares to challenge God to give a direct answer to the questions. The juristic forms of speech in this introduction have the intent of thrusting the interrogative queries directly into the presence of God. The accusation against God is transferred to an arena wherein the one asked about the legal basis must render an answer. Therefore the questions in vv. 23–27 are in fact something new over against the similarly worded questions in the preceding speeches. One does not recognize this fact if one views the Job-dialogue from a strictly conceptual perspective. All the individual questions in 13:23–27 have already been encountered; why should they have here a meaning different from the one they had in chap. 3 or chaps. 6–7 or chaps. 9–10? That this passage (13:23–27) represents a turning point in the accusation against God, and therefore also a turning point in the whole Job-drama, can be seen only under the presupposition that the whole of this drama has grown out of preexistent forms of speech. And yet, this assertion about the pivotal character of 13:23–27 can also be supported on the basis of textual observations. The extensive introduction to this preliminary inquiry of God shows that 13:23–27 is meant to be particularly emphasized, as already mentioned; nowhere else does such an extensive introduction occur. Furthermore, there is the deliberate characterizing in vv. 17–19 of what follows as a legal proceeding. On top of that, there is the character of the words in vv. 23–27 themselves: in contrast to the broad development of the accusation against God in the preceding chapters, 13:23–27 combines in stark concentration the various points of accusation contained in the previous speeches of Job, just as is done in a written indictment. The way in which accusation against God is usually divided into interrogative query (vv. 23–25) and declarative statement (vv. 26–27) occurs here as well, just as does the conjunction of (1) God's not forgiving Job (vv. 23, 26) and (2) God's acting hostilely toward Job (vv. 24, 27). As is lacking nowhere else in any previous accusation against God, so also here reference to finitude—the grounds for action—stands at the midpoint (v. 25). This concentration of themes in such clear articulation cannot be accidental!

The fourteenth chapter places this summoning of God against the background of universal human fate, which is characterized by finitude (14:1–6) and hopelessness (14:7–12). These traits are tied in with the accusation against God at 14:3 and 14:19b, at both of which places God is reproached by means of these marks of human existence. The concluding accusation then follows in v. 20: You, O God, forcibly subdue mankind and bring it to nought!

From here on one can no longer expect to find a simple continuance of the accusation against God through repetition of the old motifs. Job 13:23–27—the comprehensive letter of indictment which ties together all the previous points of accusation, throws them up before God, and now demands a divine response—has about it the character of finality and conclusiveness. The accusation against God has now—that is, at the end of the first cycle of discourse—come around to a definite conclusion. The same sort of accusation against God no longer occurs in the fourth, fifth, and sixth speeches of Job. In its place the fourth and fifth speeches contain laments about enemies which are applied to God by extension (16:9-14 and 19:7-12). God has not answered the questions put before him in 13:23-27; he has not intervened. Now Job has to assume that God is his enemy. To be sure, Job had already referred to God as an enemy in isolated clauses in his earlier accusations. However, the situation is essentially different in his fourth and fifth speeches; here the third component of the lament, which otherwise has the enemies of the lamenter as its subject, refers to God as the enemy.[70]

The Fourth and Fifth Speeches of Job, Chapters 16-17 and 19

Support for what has just been said is to be found first of all in the fact that, in distinction to both the preceding speeches, the element of accusation against God retreats fully into the background in chaps. 16-17. Only 16:9-14 is accusation against God; in essence this passage is akin to the genre of the lament about enemies.[71] The third person singular pronominal suffix in the first clause in v. 9 (*'appô*) apparently means that Job is here speaking of God. However, the verbs which follow do not fit in well with this subject; they presuppose some beast of prey as the subject. This is the kind of speech one finds in laments about enemies.[72] The reference to gnashing of teeth in the second stichos of v. 9 has precise parallels in the laments about enemies in the Psalter.[73] This imagery is probably carried on in v. 12. In v. 13 the imagery passes from that of a wild beast to that of a hostile warrior; v. 13b perhaps alludes to Job's disease. Verse 14 depicts a hostile army doing battle against a city.

Job 19:7-12 is also an accusation against God cast in the form of a lament about enemies and introduced in v. 7 by means of a self-lament. Job laments that he receives no answer and that justice is denied him.[74] Here Job states why he must now regard God as his enemy; this expresses openly what was intimated in the cry for help in Job's preceding speech (16:18). The self-lament obviously refers back to chap. 13 and further confirms that a real turning point lies

55

there. Verse 8 says that God has put up barricades in the way of the lamenter; this particular lament has found its most definitive form of expression in Lam. 3:5–9. The parallelism between Job 19:7–12 and Lamentations 3 is unmistakable.[75] In both places the realization that God has turned inimical underlies this terrifying lament: "The Lord has become like an enemy" (Lam. 2:5).[76] In the individual lament psalms one of the most frequent images of an enemy's attack against the lamenter is that of the setting up of nets; in v. 6b God's actions against Job are described in just this way! The "walling up" in v. 8 and the violating in v. 9 likewise depict God's actions against Job. The passage ends with the same image as 16:9–14, an image which blatantly expresses the hopeless supremacy of God: God brings Job down as a hostile army levels a city (vv. 10–12). All this makes the brusque transition to the avowal of trust in 19:23–27 just that much more powerful. Despite his awareness of most extreme alienation from God, Job nonetheless throws himself directly upon God.

In the sixth speech of Job (chap. 21), nothing really corresponds to the element of accusation against God.

The Seventh Speech of Job, Chapters 23–24

Here one cannot talk of a distinct accusation against God. The introductory verse is a self-lament; the nouns *complaint* and *groaning* are to be seen as standing in parallel relationship:

> Today also my complaint is "bitter,"
> "his" hand lies heavily upon my groaning.[77]

"His hand lies heavily upon me" is a related clause characteristic of accusation against God. This beginning of Job's final speech stands very close to his first speech in 6:2–4. There follows in 23:3–12 Job's expressed wish to encounter God, allied with an asseveration of innocence (vv. 7a, 10–12).[78]

Job 23:13 is thoroughly understandable as a continuation of 23:3–12. The "but he" stands in contrast to the asseveration of innocence: God does not concern himself about guilt or innocence; he merely decides, and what he decides then happens.[79] This sentence is really praise of God.[80] We have already encountered, in 10:13–19, this phenomenon whereby something which the community joyfully sings about gets turned into precisely its opposite for Job. In the presence of this God, Job can only be terrified (v. 15).[81]

From here on out everything is uncertain.[82] Only v. 16 is accusation against God in the strict sense.[83] Here the verse stands totally isolated; it would fit in better with the introduction, right after v. 2. In any case, it is uncertain in its present location. Just as doubtful is v. 17, the text of which is emended by most modern commentators;[84] at any rate, the verse is a self-lament. If the progression of the text at the conclusion has been correctly transmitted, then one can assume that the conclusion (vv. 16–17) turns back once again to the beginning (v. 2). Yet difficulties remain. The last verse which seemed to us quite certain in its context was v. 13. It is actually praise of God. We are reminded of 12:7–10 and 13 where, in the course of the conversation, Job comes upon a sentence in praise of God and then develops it in the following verses. Likewise, we must reckon here with the possibility that after 23:13 there follows a development on the theme of God's actions (he carries out what he has decided upon). However, there remains another possibility which is even more appropriate. Duhm draws attention to the fact that 23:15 recalls 21:6. This latter verse serves to introduce an argument by which Job (only in this speech!) disputes the thesis of his friends. Job himself is terrified by his argument (21:6), and he calls upon his friends to participate in his dismay (21:5). The argument advanced with such trepidation begins as "Why do the wicked live?" (21:7). There is a precise correspondence in the way 24:1 follows upon 23:15.

Now, one can isolate a group of verses from chap. 24 which correspond precisely to the speech of Job in chap. 21. This group is comprised of 24:1–4, 9, 12, 21–23, 25. The interrogative query of 24:1 asks why God does not judge transgressors. This question is then elaborated upon; first Job describes the deeds of the transgressors (vv. 2–4, 9, 12a, 12b, 21), and then he juxtaposes to these the unfathomable response of God: God even assists the transgressors (vv. 22–23)! The conclusion is formed by the polemical question in v. 25.[85]

Note that chap. 21 is unique among the speeches of Job. Only here does Job argue in the same way as his friends. Job 24:1ff. can indeed follow directly upon 23:15. However, it can hardly follow upon 23:2-13, which is in every way likely and admissible as an introduction to a speech by Job after the accusation by Eliphaz in chap. 22. It is very unlikely, on the other hand, that *after* chap. 22 Job would continue to argue in the same way as he had in chap. 21, as though nothing had happened or—to put it in other words—as though 24:1ff. were a direct continuation of chap. 21 after the interruption occasioned by the speech of Eliphaz in chap. 22. The clear structure recognized up to this point allows this to be said with certainty. Thus it is most probable that 23:15 and 24:1-4, 9, 21-25 comprise a fragment having its proper place in chap. 21. We will intentionally omit attempting to fit this fragment precisely into chap. 21. From chap. 24 on, there have been transmitted to us only fragments, unhewn building blocks which are no longer to be worked into the overall edifice. All we can any longer say is where these blocks properly belong; an attempt at reconstruction will not be possible for us.

In any case, it is at least clear that the query in 24:1 is not a direct accusation against God; it is rather a question directed to the friends, just as is 21:7.[86] The whole passage in 24:1ff. is at best only indirectly an accusation against God; essentially it is a counterargument directed against the friends, as is the whole of chap. 21. This continues to hold true even if the assumption is not adopted that in 24:1ff. we are dealing with a fragment belonging after chap. 21.

Thus there remains of chap. 24 the following: (1) a description of a group of refugees,[87] vv. 5-11 (except v. 9); (2) the enemies of the light (written in the style of Proverbs), vv. 13-17; (3) a fragment about the end of the transgressors (as this motif appears in the speeches of the friends), vv. 18-20, 24.

The Concluding Lament of Job, Chapters 29-31

The accusation against God already reached its high point in chaps. 9-10. In chaps. 12-14 it was transformed into a summoning of God (13:17-23), and in both the ensuing speeches of Job (chaps. 16-17 and 19) it took on the form of a lament about enemies. The accusation against God in the concluding lament of Job (30:18-23) ties in directly here and expresses what already was to be ascertained from the progression of themes in the speeches of Job: God has not answered Job (30:20, cf. 19:7), and so Job must assume that God has irrevocably become his enemy. "Thou hast turned cruel to me; with the might of thy hand thou dost persecute me" (30:21). These two verses, 20 and 21, stand in the midst of a final, frightful accusation against God, an accusation in which God is nothing more than the hostile demon who gives Job over to the powers of the deep (vv. 18–19[88]) and of the heights (v. 22) in order to have Job annihilated (v. 23).

It is precisely the wording of this final piece of accusation against God in 30:18–23, with its obvious references to the preceding passages, which makes it impossible to dispute the thesis of a deliberate structuring of individual motifs throughout all the speeches of Job.

NOTES

1. Cf. Claus Westermann, "Struktur und Geschichte der Klage im Alten Testament," *Zeitschrift für die alttestamentliche Wissenschaft* 66 (1954): 44–80.

2. Cf. Aage Bentzen, *Introduction to the Old Testament* (Copenhagen: G. E. C. Gad, [2]1952), 2:9.

3. Cf., *inter alia,* Lindblom, who calls 9:17–18, 25–28a "a description of the misery of Job in the style of a poem of lamentation" (Johannes Lindblom, *La composition du livre Job* [Lund: C. W. K. Gleerup, 1945], p. 53); cf. his similar evaluation of the conclusion to chap. 10, to chap. 14, and elsewhere. But what does it mean to call something a description "in the style of . . ."? What else can it mean but that these sentences are themselves lament? Stummer employs the phrase "description of misery" as a characterization of the lament in the corpus of Babylonian psalms of lamentation (Friedrich Stummer, *Sumerisch-Akkadische Parallelen zum Aufbau alttestamentlicher Psalmen* [Paderborn, 1922]); cf. Westermann, "Struktur," p. 60.

4. This comes out very emphatically in the concluding section of Baumgärtel's work. Here the Book of Job is really recognized and characterized in its essentials, and I concur with the conclusion to Baumgärtel's work without hesitation. It remains very much an open question, however, whether the determination of the structure is to be worked out as Baumgärtel does it on the basis of this conclusion, or whether it doesn't instead lie closer to the heart of the matter to interpret the whole from the *process* of lamentation (cf. Friedrich Baumgärtel, *Der Hiobdialog: Aufriss und Deutung,* Beiträge zur Wissenschaft vom Alten und Neuen Testament 61 [Stuttgart, 1933], pp. 187–88).

5. The designation "monologue" for the lament of Job at the beginning and at the end of the dialogue section should be totally abandoned. The concept of monologue is simply wide of the mark when dealing with the Book of Job. The concept is so fixed and so narrowly tied to a completely distinct mentality, one which is far removed from the Book of Job, that it would be better for this concept to be avoided here. Job no more holds forth in a monologue than does God in, say, chaps. 38–41.

6. Westermann, "Struktur," pp. 46–47.

7. Curt Kuhl, "Neuere Literarkritik des Buches Hiob," *Theologische Rundschau,* N.F. 21 (1953): 286.

8. Cf. v. 14 with Job 10:20–21!

9. On v. 4a,b cf. Ps. 38:2[3] and Deut. 32:23–24. On v. 4c cf. Ps. 88:16[17]. On v. 7 cf. Ps. 107:18. On v. 13 cf. Ps. 7:2[3]; 22:11b[12b]; 71:11; Sir. 51:7. On vv. 15–20 cf. Jer. 15:18; Ps. 41:6, 9[7, 10]; 55:12–14 [13–15].

10. Otto Eissfeldt comes to the same conclusion; cf. his *The Old Testament: An Introduction,* trans. Peter R. Ackroyd (New York: Harper & Row, 1965), pp. 464–65.

11. In v. 24; this is based upon a particular sort of suffering, namely, suffering without letup, as described in vv. 25–26.

12. The motivation clause in v. 10 has only explicative character; all it does is state more precisely what the malediction in v. 3 already said. Verses 4–9 thematicize upon the verb of the clause in v. 3. One also notes here the varying of the direct object of these sentences, solely as conditioned by the needs of the poetic parallelism. The malediction is a single sentence which has grown into such an extensive composition only in and through the effect of being a poetic composition. It is actually an independent form of speech which has been secondarily combined with the lament. The same sort of combination is found in the lament of Jeremiah (Jer. 20:14–18). The two passages are remarkably similar to one another, coinciding in almost every respect:

Jer. 20	Job 3
v. 14	3
15	3b
	4, 3a, 6a, 9 (continuation)
	4b
16b	5
16a	6b, 7, 8
17	10
18	11 (with 13–19)

It is by no means necessary to assume a literary dependence of one passage upon the other. The completely similar structure in both passages indicates a fixed preliterary form which consisted of only malediction and motivation clause. The form was here and there varied and expanded. One can say that the basic format is more developed in Job than in Jeremiah; one can also assume that the form in Job is more recent. However, none of that is certain; it would not be impossible for the two passages to be contemporary.

13. Cf. the superscription in v. 2!

14. Job 3:11-12 (expanded in vv. 13-19) corresponds to Jer. 20:18, where the original form of the self-lament is much more obvious than it is in Job 3:11-12. It is the primordial individual lament, which one encounters twice as a lament of Rebekah in the patriarchal stories (cf. Westermann, "Struktur," p. 67, and the examples there cited), Gen. 25:22 (J) and 27:46(J). It is noteworthy that both the malediction and this form of the self-lament were not taken up into the Psalter; they were too untamed to allow for incorporation into the prayer book of the community.

15. This form-critical determination makes it more obvious from the outset why the friends must react in a disputatious manner. It is not the thoughts of Job which shock them so, but rather this long since outworn, ancient, untamed form of lament which breaks forth from the mouth of Job.

16. Cf. Hermann Gunkel and Joachim Begrich, *Einleitung in die Psalmen* (Göttingen, 1933), pp. 194, 251.

17. E.g., Ps. 5, 7, 17, 26.

18. Job 27:2-6 should probably immediately precede these introductory verses.

19. Cf. Gunkel and Begrich, *Einleitung,* p. 251: "The asseveration of innocence ensues from time to time . . . in the extraordinarily impressive form of a conditioned self-vilification: Ps. 7:3-5[4-6]. Job 31:5-40 is constructed in a corresponding fashion." Köhler writes: "This is the conditional self-cursing of the accused, who thereby seeks to prove his innocence before the legal assembly" (Ludwig Köhler, "Justice in the Gate," postscript to *Hebrew Man,* trans. Peter R. Ackroyd [London: SCM, 1956], p. 160). On the relationship to the negative confessions from Egypt cf. Paul Humbert, *Recherches sur les sources égyptiennes de la littérature sapientale d'Israel,* Mémoires de l'Université de Neuchâtel 7 (Neuchâtel, 1929), pp. 91ff. Cf. also Hans Schmidt, *Das Gebet des Angeklagten im Alten Testament,* Beihefte zur Zeitschrift für die alttestamentliche Wissenschaft 49 (Giessen, 1928).

20. These clauses can either precede or (usually) follow the petition; cf. the early example at Amos 7:2.

21. Ps. 4:1[2]; 86:1; 102:2[3]; 119:145, 149; 143:1.

22. Cf. also Ps. 44:1-8[2-9], preceding the lament which begins in v. 9[10].

23. This contrast is part of the lament already in its earliest forms, e.g., Josh. 7:7-9 and Judg. 15:18.

24. The original order must have been disturbed in this chapter; this is shown especially by v. 21, with its unexpected use of plural verb forms.

25. This correspondence holds true even though the individual lament psalms refer not to enemies but to a hostile environment. While 30:9-15

(the actions of the enemies) says of the enemies precisely what is also said of them in the individual lament psalms, the section about the existence of the enemies in 30:2–8 is without any parallel. Verses 2–8 describe a despised group of wasteland inhabitants. In this context the description of this population has an ironic sense: these lowliest of the low can now poke scorn at Job! All this is a descriptive expansion upon the subject of v. 1. Within the context of the lament, v. 9 could just as well follow directly upon v. 1. But just because the "now" (wəʿattāh) of v. 1 is taken up again in v. 9, it is not to be assumed that this descriptive section was inserted at a later date. It could just as well be one of those descriptive expansions we also encounter elsewhere in the Book of Job (e.g., 3:14–19!). Now if vv. 9–15 are fully in keeping with Old Testament tradition at this point, one can assume the same for vv. 2–8. Since one finds no trace of precisely such an element elsewhere in the Old Testament, it is possible that our poet took over this small, self-contained description of an expelled group of people from a tradition rooted in the region in which our poet set the persons of the Job-drama. Eissfeldt has made this assumption very probable: "Our understanding of this in many regards obscure section of Job (30:1–8) is decisively furthered if we view it in the light of the Safa inscription, regardless of whether the reference found there to despised people, dwelling in shelters unfit for human habitation and scarcely maintaining themselves like animals, is to be understood as referring to gypsylike rabble that has penetrated the area from a desolate place neighboring on the region where Job lived, or. . ." (Otto Eissfeldt, "Das Alte Testament im Lichte der safatenischen Inschriften," *Zeitschrift der Deutschen Morganländischen Gesellschaft* 104 [1954]: 109 [= *Kleine Schriften,* ed. Rudolf Sellheim and Fritz Maass (Tübingen: J. C. B. Mohr [Paul Siebeck], 1966), 3:309]).

26. Cf. Westermann, "Struktur," p. 61.

27. Cf. Ps. 7:13; 11:2; 37:14; 57:5; 59:8; 64:3–4; 27:3; 22:20[21]. None of these citations is an exact parallel to Job 30:12–14; the images in the psalms are strongly stylized, whereas the picture in Job 30:12–14 is realistically painted. But the introductory sentence in v. 12, "Against me there arise. . . ," shows that the same motif is being employed; cf., e.g., Ps. 27:3b and 13:3–4.

28. This was correctly seen by Baumgärtel (*Hiobdialog,* pp. 131–32).

29. Ibid.

30. A close parallel to 30:9 is found in Lam. 3:14; one finds both the verbs in this verse also in Job 30:1, 9. The closest parallel to Job 30:11 is Job 19:13, 19. General verbs of scorning are rare in the individual lament psalms, where concrete verbs predominate. Psalm 4:2 resembles v. 11. Even if the verbs "make sport of" (śḥq) and "abhor" (tʿb) do not exactly fit the behavior of the friends toward Job, the friends have now finally become for Job what the transgressors, the "ungodly," are for the laments in Psalms. In using these clauses, Job stands in harmony with the lament about enemies as voiced before him, contemporary with him, and even after him.

31. That God is initially referred to in the third person but then from v. 20 on is addressed directly is by no means an impossibility; this unmotivated change from the second to the third person or vice versa frequently occurs in the psalms in the praise of God, in avowals of trust in God, and in accusations against God. In my opinion Baumgärtel (and others) makes too much of this change in person.

32. A frequently voiced lament; cf. Ps. 22:2[3] and the "negative petitions" ("be not silent!"); cf. also Ps. 28:1; 39:12[13]; 35:22; 109:1[2].

33. The image goes on to include the notion of active persecution; cf. v. 21b. The verb śṭm ("to persecute"), with reference to God, is also found in 16:9 (however, the text is uncertain).

34. This poetically appealing correspondence between the two processes would have been more apparent if v. 20 could have been read before vv. 18-19.

35. Cf. Ps. 88:6[7] and 102:10[11].

36. An asseveration of innocence stands in the middle (v. 25); following this verse is a clause about the futility of hope, while preceding it is a verse which has the character of a transitional device. The clause about the futility of hope has parallels in the communal lament psalms: cf. Jer. 13:16; 14:19 = 8:15; Isa. 59:9, 11; Ps. 69:20[21]. In all these other places, the clause about futility of hope is conjoined with a confession of sins; in Job it is conjoined with an asseveration of innocence. Both the confession of sins and the asseveration of innocence have the same function within the context of the lament, namely, to motivate God to act. Verse 25 is also meant to be taken in much the same way.

37. Particularly close parallels are found in Lam. 1:20-22 and 2:10-11; cf. also Ps. 38:6, 8, 10 [7, 9, 11].

38. The comparison with the parallels leads to the conclusion that one must give up attempts at proposing deletions or alterations to the text on the basis of some putative logical connection between the elements in this text. (1) For example, Karl Budde (*Das Buch Hiob*, Handkommentar zum Alten Testament 2/1 [Göttingen, ²1913]) wishes to strike out (v. 27 and) v. 30 because the lament about illness does not belong in this context. A glance at Psalm 38 is enough to discredit Budde's suggestion. In Psalm 38 the laments about illness are so scattered throughout the psalm without any logical connection (vv. 3, 5, 7, 8a, 10b [4, 6, 8, 9a, 11b]) that the placing of v. 30 in Job 30 is readily justifiable. (2) Duhm's suggestion, namely, that in v. 28 the unintelligible ḥmh is perhaps to be read as nəḥāmāh ("comfort") (Bernhard Duhm, *Das Buch Hiob*, Kurzer Handkommentar zum Alten Testament 16 [Freiburg, 1897]; most modern exegetes follow Duhm's suggestion), is confirmed by the parallel in Lam. 1:21. (3) Conversely, in Ps. 38:8[9] it has been proposed to read lāḇî' ("lion") in place of the final word, libbî ("my heart"). This proposal is confirmed by the precise correspondence between Job 30:28, 29 and Ps. 38:6, 8 [7, 9].

On the whole the parallels show that an unambiguous connection between the clauses in this section of the self-lament can no longer be reconstructed by us. We could neither postulate the correct sequence for these clauses nor say with certainty what is lacking or what must be added. In the case of this self-lament, we are obviously dealing with a severely garbled theme. Perhaps there once was a fixed form with a recognizable sequence of individual motifs; however, this is no longer accessible to us. Thus one will have to accept the text as it has been transmitted to us.

39. However, the psalm of lamentation would not conclude with a petition. Something else must still follow the petition, which here in Job is so intensified as to be a summoning. On the basis of the structure of the psalms of lamentation, this something could only be an oracle promising salvation, or some corresponding element (cf. Joachim Begrich, "Das priesterliche Heilsorakel," *Zeitschrift für die alttestamentliche Wissenschaft* 52 [1934]: 81-92).

40. Moreover, this is simply not possible until the themes of the lament in the psalms have been comprehensively described in their original compositional structure. Even the *Einleitung* by Gunkel and Begrich does not go beyond a mere listing here. In my study on the lament, I have attempted to present the outline of such a comprehensive description of the lament.

41. Ps. 41:9[10]; 35:13-15; 27:10; 38:11[12]; 88:8[9], 18[19]; cf. Gunkel and Begrich, *Einleitung,* sec. 6, 9.

42. Ps. 31:11[12]; 35:12-14; 38:19[20]; 69:8-12[9-13]; 109:4.

43. See also Ps. 27:10; 31:11[12]; 88:8[9], 18[19]; Jer. 12:6; 20:10; cf. Gunkel and Begrich, *Einleitung,* p. 211.

44. Cf. Lindblom, *La composition,* p. 93.

45. Job 17:4-10, which might possibly belong here, is nonetheless very questionable.

46. Cf. Ps. 86:1; 88:3[4]; 40:12[13]; 102:3.

47. Cf. also Ps. 31:10[11]; 13:2[3].

48. Job 7:4 obviously points back to 3:26.

49. A lament about disease appears one more time, in 19:20, 27c. But both times here the lament appears so abruptly alongside other motifs that both instances must remain open to question.

50. Cf. George Widengren, *The Accadian and Hebrew Psalms of Lamentation as Religious Documents: A Comparative Study* (Uppsala, 1936).

51. The origin in the lament is particularly obvious in Ps. 13:3b[4b]; cf. Ps. 28:1b; 88:3[4], expanded in vv. 4-6[5-7]; 102:24[25]; 62:9b; 39:5-8, 12.

52. Note the recurrence of this motif at the end of the chapter, in v. 21b.

53. In the rest of chaps. 9-10, the self-lament occurs only in individual clauses within accusations against God; cf. 9:17-18 and the last lines of 9:31 and 9:35. In chap. 10 true self-lament is found only in the clause in v. 1a; as a rule the accusation against God is framed by the self-lament, but of that framework here only one clause remains. Cf. the corresponding transition in 7:10. In 10:8-17 self-lament is to be found only in the one stichos at v. 15b.

54. Right at the end of the third speech, it is hinted that this so persistent

process of generalization still has its origin in the self-lament: in 14:10-17, where Job once again speaks in the first person, and in the two final verses (21, 22), which obviously echo with the self-lament.

55. This is especially obvious in 17:16: hope and happiness together go down into Sheol.

56. The precise determination of the motif is difficult because the text is disrupted. It is certain that 16:15-16 belongs to this motif, while 17:7 and the textually uncertain 17:2 probably do too.

57. In the fifth speech of Job, only the one sentence at 19:7 hints at self-lament. Job laments that he receives no answer from God. The sentence serves as the introduction to the accusation against God in vv. 7-12. The clause at 19:27c is only fragmentarily preserved; the same applies to 23:17—a sentence which could be a self-lament but which is textually very uncertain.

58. Cf. Westermann, "Struktur," pp. 52-53.

59. Job 7:17 is also really a motif from the praise of God; here we see a deliberately ironic citation of Ps. 8:4[5].

60. Cf. Job 38:8-11; Ps. 104:9; Jer. 5:22.

61. The same Hebrew root is employed in both places (*b't*).

62. E.g., Ps. 74:1, 10; 80:4, 12[13]; Hab. 1:2-3. The two questions do not occur together in the same psalm in any of the individual lament psalms.

63. A similar theme, though not pushed to such a radical conclusion, occurs in Lam. 1:14a: "He has 'watched over' my sins."

64. Job 10:1 is the transition from self-lament to accusation against God. The petition in v. 2a is very striking: "Do not condemn me!" Indeed, Job has already said that he feels himself to be one pronounced guilty by God (9:20-31). It is possible that the text is disrupted and that a "why" (*lāmmāh*) is to be read in place of the "not" (*'al*). Thereby the first stichos would parallel the second, and the difficulty would be overcome.

65. The word used here (*rîb*) has its proper setting in the genre of prophetic accusation.

66. The intervening vv. 4-7 raise the question of why God, who is eternal and sees all (vv. 4-5), investigates as he does the sins of Job even though he must know that Job is innocent (tying in with 9:21-23). The second stichos of v. 7 is questionable; Duhm takes a clue from 21:34 and reads: "and no deceit clings to my hand" (*wə'ên bəyādî mā'al*).

67. Many commentaries remark upon this.

68. Cf. Köhler, "Justice," and Stier: "Chap. 13 is a reservoir of jurisprudential terminology" (Fridolin Stier, *Das Buch Ijjob, hebräisch und deutsch* [Munich: Kosel, 1954], p. 289).

69. Deutero-Isaiah frequently imitates this form of speech.

70. See pp. 43-46, above, on the lament about enemies.

71. The text of the whole speech in 16:9-14 is badly disrupted. Verses 9b, 10, 11 are probably interpolations, so originally v. 12 followed immedi-

ately after v. 9a (cf. Samuel R. Driver and George Buchanan Gray, *The Book of Job,* International Critical Commentary 10, 11 [Edinburgh, 1921]).

72. E.g., "They are like a lion eager to tear" (Ps. 17:12) or "like a ravening and roaring lion" (Ps. 22:13[14]); in both places the verb *ṭrp* is used, just as in Job 16:9a. The appropriateness of the vague, general "and hated me" (*wayyiśṭəmēnî*) in Job 16:9a has properly been questioned. Duhm *(Das Buch Hiob),* Gustav Hölscher *(Das Buch Hiob,* Handbuch zum Alten Testament 1/17 [Tübingen: J. C. B. Mohr (Paul Siebeck), ²1952]), and others propose the emendation "and threw me down" (*wayyišmaṭēnî*).

73. Cf. Ps. 35:16b; 37:12.

74. Cf. Ps. 22:2[3]; Isa. 40:27.

75. On v. 8a cf. Lam. 3:7; on v. 8b cf. Lam. 3:6, 2; on v. 7 cf. Lam. 3:8; on v. 9 cf. Lam. 3:14; on v. 11 cf. Lam. 3:43. Verse 9b appears word-for-word in Lam. 5:16a; v. 10a in Lam. 2:2; v. 11a in Lam. 2:40; v. 11b in Lam. 2:5a.

76. Cf. Job 19:6, 11, 21b, 22a.

77. Read "bitter" (*mar*) in place of the text's "rebellious" (*mərî*) and "his hand" (*yāḏô*) in place of the text's "my hand" (*yāḏî*).

78. Verses 8–9 are probably an interpolation; cf. Driver and Gray, *Job.*

79. Read "he chooses" (*bāḥar*) in place of the text's "unchangeable" (*bə'eḥāḏ*); this emendation is rendered probable by comparison with Ps. 132:13, where "chooses" (*bāḥar*) stands parallel with "desires" (*'iwwāh*).

80. Cf. Ps. 33:9 and 132:13–14.

81. In a prophetic context one encounters the theme of terror in the presence of God's decree; cf. Isa. 19:16–17.

82. Verse 14 is allowable if translated in strict accordance with the context. However, the verse presents many difficulties; cf. Driver and Gray, *Job.* This verse is lacking in the Septuagint; Hölscher also takes it out.

83. The copula (*w*) at the beginning of v. 16 presents difficulties; it is left untranslated in the RSV.

84. With Hölscher I strike the "not" (*lō'*) in the first stichos and the "from" (*min*) in the second stichos; the "for" (*kî*) at the beginning is hard to understand after v. 16.

85. The context would then have to be indicated at the beginning of v. 22, perhaps by "but he" (*wəhû'*), if indeed v. 21 did not originally follow directly upon v. 12c, where just such an expression ("yet God" [*we'ĕlôah*]) occurs. If the latter were the case, then it would mean that v. 12 also belongs to this section.

86. By the way, in both places "why" is expressed by *maddûa'* not by *lāmmāh*!

87. Cf. Eissfeldt, "Das Alte Testament im Lichte," p. 35, n. 3.

88. We read vv. 18–19 following the translation of Hölscher; Kissane reads the same (Edward J. Kissane, *The Book of Job* [New York: Sheed & Ward, 1946]).

4

Wishes and Petitions in the Speeches of Job

In our investigation here, we have undertaken the attempt to understand the Book of Job in terms of its structure, as this is determined from the forms of speech employed in the book. Let us now turn to an examination of the element of petition, a form which is easily recognized as such and which can be identified with certainty. Petition, or at any rate something like petition, intrinsically belongs to the lament. The mere presence of a lament can already imply a petition.[1] Or we can have a situation such as we have in the Book of Job, where the element of petition has moved far into the background and appears—where it still does appear—almost solely in the attenuated form of a mere wish. And yet, every lament contains within itself an inclination toward petition. Hence even those few petitions and wishes which do appear in the Book of Job must be important for the structure of the whole.

In fact, the petitions and wishes display an evident and quite unmistakable way of fitting into the overall structure of the Book of Job. All in all, the petitions and wishes encountered in the speeches of Job can be arranged into four groups (of which the third and fourth are much alike). These four groups coincide almost totally with the sections of the Book of Job; they are as follows:

1. The wish to die (3:11–13, 21–22; 6:8–10; 7:15; an echo of this wish occurs in 10:18b–19)
2. The wish that God would leave Job alone
    a) so that Job might be able to breathe freely (7:16b; 10:20b)

    or so that mankind might be able to breathe freely (14:6,
13-15)

    b) so that Job might be able to address God (9:34-35;
13:21-22 [and hear God's answer])

3. The wish that Job's cause might be heard and that he might
find an advocate despite his death (16:18-22; 17:3; 19:23-24)

4. The wish to encounter God (23:3-12; 31:35-37 [the summoning of God])

1. Job's wish to die arises directly out of the cry at the beginning.
This is the wish of a person in most extreme agony, the wish of one
who can hold out no longer. To be sure, this wish is not openly
stated in the introductory lament, but it is implied above all in
3:11-13 (referring to Job himself) and in 3:21-22 (referring to
anonymous sufferers). The wish is emphatically expressed in Job's
first speech, in 6:8-10. In the same speech, in 7:15, Job says indirectly that he would choose to die. The same wish echoes once more
from a distance in 10:18b-19. The decrescendo from chap. 3 to
chap. 10 can clearly be perceived. This particular wish does not
subsequently occur.

2. Immediately following the wish to die in his first speech, at
7:15, Job gives voice to another wish, which actually contradicts
the first: "Leave me alone!" This latter wish shows up in all three
speeches in the first cycle of discourse: in the first speech, at 7:16b;
in the second, at 10:20b; in the third, at 14:6 (referring to mankind
in general). According to our understanding, this wish to be left
alone means the same as wishing to be left in peace. Therefore this
second wish is also a very basic sort of petition which comes directly out of living under a state of oppression. At all three places,
this petition stands in association with the lament about transitoriness: "Leave me alone, for my days are a breath!" (7:16b). In the
first and the second speeches, one also finds in the same context
that invocation of God which resembles a petition and which serves
to stimulate action: Remember the frailty of mankind! (7:7 and
10:9). Our petition reappears in 14:13-15 in singular transformation; here Job beseeches God to leave him alone for a set length of
time in the future. This is also where, for the first time, the petition
leads to a wish for a direct encounter with God (v. 15).

This same petition, namely, that God might leave Job alone, also appears in the first cycle of discourse in a different context. Job also expresses the wish that God might leave off striking him with his blows so that he might have a chance to speak to God (9:34–35) and be able to hear God's answer (13:21–22; cf. also 13:3). Both these optative lines of thought terminate in the wish for a direct encounter with God (13:21–22 and 14:15). But this latter wish gets developed only in the third cycle of discourse.

3. The wish is for something else in the second cycle of discourse. This is the cycle in which the accusation against God became a lament about enemies—in Job's fourth and fifth speeches, at any rate. In both these speeches the wish is almost the same. In a wish logically incompatible with the first, Job implores that his cause be heard and carried through to a resolution despite his death. This wish is allied with an avowal of trust in both places where it occurs.

4. Only in the third cycle of discourse, in the seventh and final speech of Job in the dialogue section, does the main wish finally stand forth in clear and unhindered fashion—the wish for a direct encounter with God. This is the real wish toward which Job has been struggling all along. This is shown by the fact that, directly after the introductory v. 2, this final speech of Job starts out by saying, "Oh, that I knew where I might find him" (23:3). Furthermore, this is the most elaborate wish in the whole Book of Job.[2] The centrality of this particular wish is emphasized even more by the way that both the optative lines of thought in the first cycle of discourse point in the direction of this wish (13:21–22 and 14:15) and by the fact that the wish for a direct encounter with God is once again taken up at the end, in the closing words of the concluding lament (31:35–37).

This final, so strongly emphasized wish in chap. 23 is to be viewed against the background of the total course of the action. The unrestrained and sweeping accusation of Job by Eliphaz precedes this final speech by Job. Job no longer responds directly to this accusation; now all there is left for him to cling to is the final court of appeal. All this stands in the background of Job's wish in 23:3–12, namely, that God might grant him a favorable hearing.

Here in 23:3–12 Job brings together all his petitions and wishes, just as he had done with all his accusations against God in

13:23-27. There are three main concerns: (1) "Oh, that I knew where I might find him." The lament about God's remoteness stands behind this wish. Job experiences this remoteness in his suffering; to find God, to draw near to him, would mean the removal of his suffering. (2) "I would lay my case before him." Here we see the line of thought which points backward to chap. 13 and forward to 31:35-37 (where it is also introduced as a wish). (3) "I would learn what he would answer me." This corresponds to the lament that Job receives no answer to his cries; it likewise points forward to 31:35-37.

The apprehension which hovers in the background of the second wish resounds once more in 23:6a, namely, that God might not permit Job to speak but instead merely beat him into silent submission. But the second sentence here, 23:6b, once again states what Job's wish really comes down to: "If only" he himself would pay heed to me! In the last analysis, all Job really wants is for God to grant him a hearing. This last sentence corresponds to the first component of the petition in the psalms, namely, the petition for God to grant a hearing.[3]

NOTES

1. This was particularly the case in the early history of the lament.

2. This holds true if one ignores for the time being the fact that the whole of chap. 29 is introduced as being a wish.

3. On the dividing of the petition in the psalms into two parts see Claus Westermann, *The Praise of God in the Psalms,* trans. Keith R. Crim (Richmond: John Knox, 1965), p. 64 (= *Das Loben Gottes in den Psalmen* (Berlin: Evangelische Verlagsanstalt, 1953), p. 44.

5

The Praise of God

As for the praise of God which occurs in the speeches of both Job and his friends, the same holds true that was said in reference to the motifs of its counterpart, the lament. It has its own life; it has its own structure, with multiple subdivisions. The individual clauses of praise of God by no means follow aimlessly one after another. Rather the basic motifs, which are the same here as the ones used to praise God in the psalms, are thoughtfully developed. Descriptive praise of God in Psalms consistently orients itself around two foci: praise of God in his majesty and praise of God in his mercy. Only praise of God in his majesty shows up in the dialogue section of the Book of Job. In Psalms, this focal point gets developed along two fronts; the majesty of God is revealed in nature (praise of God the creator), and it is also shown by the course of history (praise of the lord of history). The same thing happens in the passages in praise of God in the Book of Job. Likewise here the broader development of both these aspects is not aimless but controlled; it follows the paths prescribed by Israelite tradition. Almost without exception we encounter the same sort of branching out in both the Book of Job and in the praise of God in Psalms. Therefore the supposition lies close at hand that the motifs of praise of God, as well as their paths of development, are not indiscriminately scattered among the speeches of Job and his friends. On the contrary, we must assume that their distribution is consciously adapted to fit in with the structure of the whole. The element of deliberateness shows up initially in the overall distribution; those passages which contain praise of God, both on the part of Job and on the part of the friends, occur almost exclusively in the first cycle of discourse. Praise of God in both its aspects is totally lacking in the second cycle of discourse. In the third cycle, several clauses in praise of God show up once again in the speech of Eliphaz (22:12, 29, 30). An essential statement gets made in this way. In the first cycle of discourse, Job and his friends still agree on one basic point; here they still have something in common: both praise God! Praise of God is affirmation of God. We will see how already in this praise of God a different tone resounds here and there. Be that as it may, however, the friends affirm God and Job affirms God. In so doing, they both are still standing on common ground. Neither party renders up any praise of God in the second cycle of discourse. Here the friends have given up trying to persuade Job to repent;[1] Job comes to the conviction that his friends have become enemies. Thus praise of God is muted on the part of both. When praise of God once again commences in the third speech of Eliphaz—just as admonition to repent likewise resurfaces here—the situation has changed. As far as Job is concerned, a different God is here being praised—not the one to whom he cried out in his despair. A chasm separates the praise of God in these two places.

The Praise of God in the Speeches of Job

The distribution of motifs in the speeches of Job is hardly aimless. One observation can be made at first glance: both branches of the praise of God in his majesty appear in the second and third speeches of Job in such a way that *only* praise of God the creator occurs in chaps. 9–10 and *only* praise of the lord of history shows up in chap. 12. In other words, the element of praise of God in his majesty is developed in the second and third speeches of the first cycle of discourse. There is probably a recognizable reason why such praise is missing in the first speech. It is not totally missing, however. In 7:12, in the midst of an accusation against God, there is a sentence reminiscent of a motif common to praise of God (see above, p. 51); 7:17 is quite obviously an ironic citation from Psalm 8; the element of address in 7:20 ("thou watcher of men") likewise goes back to a motif of praise of God.[2] Here in his first speech, Job is so deeply into lamentation (the self-lament) that the element of praise of God is still overwhelmed by the lament; only occasionally does a glimmer of praise shine through.

A detailed look at the praise of God in the second and third speeches reveals the following structure:

	Second Speech	Third Speech
Praise of God in His Majesty	9:4, 10, 11	12:10, 13
Praise of the Creator	9:5-13 + 10:8-12	———
Praise of the Lord of History	———	12:14-25

The praise of the creator in the second speech is developed like this:[3]

9:8-9—the creator of heaven (and the sea) and the stars
9:5-7—the lord of his creation, who can move the created order at will
9:12-13—the lord of his creation, who can also destroy
10:8-12—the creator of mankind

The praise of the lord of history in the third speech is developed like this:

12:10—he is the lord of all mankind[4]
12:23—he exalts the peoples, and he destroys them (the lord of history!)
12:14-16—God's work of destruction in the realm of history (analogous to his activity in the realm of creation, v. 15)
12:17-25—he overthrows the great and the mighty (analogous to his activity in the realm of creation, v. 22)

Both groups follow a similar pattern in the way they develop the overall theme of the praise of God in his majesty.

These motifs are developed in the same way as in the psalms of praise in the Psalter. Thus also in these passages where he praises God, Job moves along traditional lines.[5] However, many interpreters have already noted how in these passages the praise of God in his majesty is deliberately developed in a one-sided fashion, emphasizing the negative aspects. This happens in different ways in different places, some quite striking. In chap. 9 the traditional praise of the creator in vv. 8-9 is expanded in a customary way: the creator is lord of his creation (vv. 5-7). But these clauses are already one-sided; what gets emphasized is the creator's ability to overturn mountains and cause the earth to quake. This theme is intensified even more in vv. 12–13. If God deals with his creation in anger, then surely no one is in a position to withstand him. In this same speech of Job, within the accusation against God, we find praise of the creator of mankind. This motif first shows up in 10:3 and is then developed in 10:8–17 in such a way that the contrast between God's creative and his destructive activity vis-à-vis his creation is clearly brought out. In the elaboration upon the creative aspect of this contrast in vv. 8–12, the motif of "the creator of mankind" is taken over directly from praise of God. The intensification as one moves from the first, fully positive words in praise of God in 9:8–9 to this defiantly uttered contrast in 10:8–17 is simply amazing.

Praise of the creator and praise of the lord of history belong together as the two antipodes along which development of the praise of God in his majesty occurs.[6] Thus the section containing praise of God in chap. 12 goes along with that in chap. 9 as two parts of the same whole. Both start out the same way, namely, by praising God in his majesty (12:10 and 13 = 9:8–9). The summarizing statement that God is the lord of history stands way at the end in chap. 12 (at v. 23). Given the pattern of development here, the stress in this summary lies on the second verb of each stichos: he destroys—he leads away. The elaboration upon this core idea in 12:14–25 is a truly magnificent depiction of the tragic in human history.[7] Just as God is the lord of his creation (9:5–7), so also is he the lord of all mankind (12:10). Because God is lord, he can also destroy (12:14–16). He controls the stream of historical events every bit as much as he does the waters of the world which he has created. He can make the waters dry up or he can turn them loose to inundate everything. Similarly he can overthrow and destroy the great, the noble, the mighty, the ones in authority—as he alone sees fit. He can cast them down into the depths, into the realm of non-being, and no one can resist him. Elsewhere, the motif "God the lord of history" is developed in a twofold manner: God exalts—God abases. The same is said in reference to the people in v. 23, but only the negative side of the picture gets developed. The particularity of the praise of God on the part of Job is shown not only in this one-sided emphasis but even more clearly in a subtle and very deliberate distinction. Where the motif of God's abasing occurs in the speeches of the friends, the friends immediately add that the ones thus abased by God are naturally the transgressors (see below)! But this is precisely what Job does *not* say. For Job the destructive activity of God does not break out against the great, the noble, the mighty—all those entrusted with authority—in any evenhanded way; it remains mysterious, incomprehensible, unfathomable. The downfall of these great figures is not deserved; it is tragic. This passage in the Book of Job is of considerable importance from the standpoint of intellectual history.

The Praise of God in the Speeches of the Friends

Given the above summarizing of the element of praise of God in the speeches of Job, one approaches the speeches of the friends in the first cycle of discourse expecting to find here as well some development of this genre. However, explicit praise of God occurs only in the first speech of Eliphaz, although a few clauses of praise also occur in the first speech of Zophar. Praise of God is totally absent in the first speech of Bildad. In the final speech of Eliphaz a few more clauses in praise of God show up once again. One must ask whether the original structure of the Book of Job has been preserved here. Which motifs from praise of God appear in the speeches of the friends, and how are these motifs distributed?

With regard to 5:9-20, in the first speech of Eliphaz, the first verse praises the God "who does great things." This corresponds to the introductory verses of praise of God in the speeches of Job in that the praise of God in his majesty is expanded upon here as well.[8] Now it is quite striking that the praise of the creator is here sung in only a single, isolated clause: "he gives rain" (v. 10). Some textual error may well lie close at hand here. The following vv. 11-16 exhibit only praise of the lord of history, developed in the traditional way: God exalts (vv. 11, 15, 16)—God abases (vv. 12, 13).[9] Thus we find the same motif and the same pattern of development that we found in the speech of Job in chap. 12. The difference between the two, however, is immediately apparent: those over-thrown by God are, for Eliphaz, the crafty (cf. 15:5, where the same word occurs), the wily—in short, all such as have no doubt deserved their demise. The difference is even more obvious at v. 14, which is indeed very similar to Job's statement at 12:25 but which here obviously echoes those clauses in which the fate of the ungodly is described. The God who is here praised in the speech of Eliphaz is a God whose actions in the realm of history can be perceived and can be evaluated according to criteria accessible to human manipu-lation. This conviction is once again expressed, much more directly and bluntly, in the final speech of Eliphaz; in 22:29-30 the praise of God is quite firmly allied with the friends' doctrine of retribution: God humbles the proud (v. 29a), but he rescues the innocent (vv. 29b, 30a). In all this the hymnic motif "God exalts—God abases" stays true to its external form, but this form is actually filled with a different content. Furthermore, in both these speeches of Eliphaz the praise of God is not voiced for its own sake; rather, it has the intention of admonishing and warning Job. This is shown in Eliphaz's first speech by the concluding admonition in 5:27. In the other speech in question, Eliphaz attaches the hymnic motif (22:29-30) to the concluding admonition (22:21-24, expanded by vv. 25-28).

The praise of God in the speech of Zophar (11:7-11) is simply a praising of God in his majesty. This praising is developed in only one particular direction: God is unfathomable (11:7-9; cf. Psalm 139). This reference to the unfathomable depth and breadth of God stands in the context of disputational discourse and follows upon the warning in 11:6b: "Know then that God exacts of you less than your guilt deserves!" Not only that, but this snippet of praise ends up in 11:11 with the clause "For he knows worthless men." Obvi-ously Zophar intends to strip Job of the illusion that he might be able to elude God by concealing his sin (cf. again Psalm 139). Once again praise of the majesty of God is totally subservient to the ulte-rior motives of the friends.[10] Once again it is apparent how praise of God, which sentence for sentence could just as conceivably stand in the mouth of Job, receives a completely different slant when placed in the context of the speeches of the friends.

If one now compares the praise of God in the speeches of Job and in those of the friends, the following picture emerges:

	JOB			FRIENDS		
	I	II	III	ELIPHAZ I	BILDAD II	ZOPHAR III
Praise of God in His Majesty		9:4, 10(?), 11	12:10, 13	5:9		11:7-9, 11
Praise of Creator of the World	(7:12)	9:5-13		(10)		
Praise of Creator of Mankind	(7:12)	10:8-12				
Praise of Lord of History	(7:12)		12:14-25	5:11-16, 18		10(?)

This overview enables us to see how very surprising it is that the speech of Bildad contains not a single motif in praise of God. If one notices in addition that the praise of the majesty of God is developed in both its customary directions in the second and third speeches of Job but that, in contrast, it is developed in only one direction—the lord of history[11]—in the speeches of the friends, then one is justified in asking whether praise of the creator is not also to be anticipated in one of the friends' speeches in this cycle of discourse. As it turns out, this expected motif of praise of the creator is contained in the Book of Job in another place, namely, in 25:2-3 and 26:5-14.[12] The latter passage contains a development of this motif, while 25:2-3 hymns the majesty of God (thereby making the correspondence even more precise). If one now inserts chaps. 25 and 26 into the schema given above, the result is a precise correspondence between the second and third speeches of Job on the one hand and the speeches of Eliphaz and Bildad on the other. Moreover, if unhewn fragments are contained in chaps. 24-27—as was demonstrated elsewhere—and the speeches of the friends conclude with the third speech of Eliphaz, then nothing stands in the way of seeing the original location of 25:2-3 and 26:5-14 in the first speech of Bildad.[13]

The text itself supports our hypothesis in several ways. First, chap. 25 is introduced as a speech of Bildad. The noticeable brevity of the chapter points in the direction of a disruption. It is most tempting to see the development of the praise of God in 26:6-14 as going with 25:2-3 (or 2-6); then the superscription in 26:1, which introduces the following as a speech of Job, would refer only to 26:1-4. The sole alteration here would then consist in transposing 26:5-14 before 26:1-4. Job 26:1-4 is without doubt the introduction to a speech of Job. If one leaves 26:1-4 in its proposed location—following immediately after 26:5-14—and then transposes the whole of chaps. 25-26 to the end of the first speech of Bildad in chap. 8, then 26:1-4 becomes the introduction to the second speech of Job in chaps. 9-10. This is a thoroughly plausible move, especially since the element of personal address in chap. 9 is noticeably short.[14] This move results in yet another surprising improvement. Currently the second speech of Job begins with an agreement with Bildad regarding the issue "How can a man be just before God?" (9:2). As it now stands, this particular argument is lacking in the speech of Bildad. However, if chaps. 25-26 (except for 26:1-4) are a part of this speech of Bildad, then precisely this argument stands immediately before the response of Job in 9:2-3.[15] This move would overcome a difficulty which has long troubled exegetes. It has been said that 9:2 refers to 8:3: "Does God pervert justice?" However, the subject matter differs in these two places. Other interpreters say that Job is referring back to the speech of Eliphaz in 4:12-21, where at least the same subject matter is being argued. This is not impossible, but it is unlikely. The passage in 4:12-21 lies too far back, and Job's words in 9:2-3 sound as though they refer to something that has just been said. Thus the situation at 9:2-3 strikes me as a significant confirmation of the argument that chaps. 25-26 comprise a fragment whose proper place is at the end of the first speech of Bildad. Furthermore, chaps. 9-10 contain no element of disputation speech, although such an element is to be found in all the other speeches of Job. Job 26:1-4 thus fits very nicely at the beginning of chap. 9.

An argument of a negative sort applies here as well. After the massive accusations of Eliphaz in chap. 22 and the silence of Job over against these accusations in chap. 23, it is most unlikely that either Job or the friends would continue to speak as they did in their earlier speeches, as though nothing had just happened. After chaps. 22 and 23, therefore, neither Job's opening remarks in

26:2-4 nor Bildad's speech in chaps. 25-26 are actually in the right place.

Difficulties remain. I cannot with certainty identify the gaps in chap. 8 into which chaps. 25-26 would fit; in fact, one cannot even say unconditionally that something is missing in chap. 8. On the other side of the coin, the complex made up of chaps. 25-26 is itself much too confused and fragmentary to allow for any certain conclusions there either. Therefore I do not maintain that one can simply transpose chaps. 25-26 after chap. 8 and leave them there. Rather with chaps. 25-26 we are dealing with an unfinished fragment. However, we can assume with a high degree of probability that the place where this fragment was intended to go lies between our present chap. 8 and chap. 9.

On the whole, this would appear to be a simple solution.[16] It yields the following result: The speech of Bildad in chap. 8 passes over—just as abruptly as does that of Eliphaz in chap. 5—into praise of God the creator, which is to be found in 25:2-3 and 26:5-14 (we can leave open the question of the proper sequence of verses here). This praise of God has a particular intent—again just like that of Eliphaz in chap. 5. The intent of Bildad's praise is to establish the argument which stands at the end of his speech: no man is righteous before God (25:4-6). With this the speech of Bildad comes to an end. Now Job answers. The first words of his answer are found in 26:2-4, upon which 9:2ff. can be appended without difficulty.

My proposed solution has the additional advantage of preserving intact both of the introductions (25:1 and 26:1). Apart from the one transposition, my solution requires no alterations or deletions.

NOTES

1. Also missing in this cycle are admonitions to repent; see above, p. 20.
2. Perhaps we should note in passing that the first hymnic allusion is in praise of the creator of the world, the second in praise of the creator of mankind, the third in praise of the lord of history.
3. Perhaps vv. 8-11 are to be read after v. 4.
4. Verses 11-12 are probably a later addition (v. 11 also occurs in 34:3).

5. Cf. Claus Westermann, *The Praise of God in the Psalms,* trans. Keith R. Crim (Richmond: John Knox, 1965), pp. 116–22 (= *Das Loben Gottes in den Psalmen* [Berlin: Evangelische Verlagsanstalt, 1953], pp. 83–87).

6. This can be seen, e.g., in the case of Psalm 33; cf. ibid., pp. 125–26 (= pp. 89–90).

7. It seems to me that this is the only place in the Bible where the concept of the tragic in its strict and proper sense can be found. Job himself is by no means a tragic figure. However, the poet of the Book of Job has recognized the tragic dimension and powerfully depicted it in these words. Insofar as these verses have grown out of the confluence of the two themes of praise of God and accusation against God, we have thereby discovered some essential roots of the tragic. The humanizing of the tragic, carried out by the poets of the Greek tragedies, lies only one step beyond this point.

8. Job 5:9 is identical to 9:10; it is possible that this verse was subsequently inserted at 9:10, though this is not necessarily the case.

9. This two-sided activity of God in history appears once more in v. 18, employed somewhat differently: "He wounds, but he binds up."

10. Job 11:10, which is very similar to 9:12, is seen as a later addition by many interpreters (e.g., Gustav Hölscher, *Das Buch Hiob,* Handbuch zum Alten Testament 1/17 [Tübingen: J. C. B. Mohr (Paul Siebeck), ²1952]). That is quite probable; nonetheless, v. 10 is by no means impossible as a development of the motif at hand (the lord of history).

11. Apart from the one clause in 5:10.

12. The fact that chaps. 25–26 are so fragmentarily preserved creates difficulties from the outset. In any case, 25:2 is certainly not a genuine beginning. Job 26:5 can hardly follow upon 26:4; 26:1–4 is undoubtedly a fragment: something must be missing before 26:5.

13. This was already suggested by Volz (*Das Buch Hiob,* Schriften des Alten Testaments 3/2 [Göttingen, 1911], pp. 34–35); Hempel agrees with him.

14. Cf. Volz, *Das Buch Hiob.*

15. Certainly the location of 25:4–6 between 25:2–3 and 26:5ff. is awkward; it would fit better after 26:14, so that it actually came right at the end of Bildad's speech and stood directly before 9:2. Given the fragmentary character of these passages, however, one cannot make any certain judgments here.

16. In any case, it is simple compared with the attempted solutions as collected by Curt Kuhl ("Neuere Literarkritik des Buches Hiob," *Theologische Rundschau,* N.F. 21 [1953]: 277–81).

6

The Arguments of the Friends

The Fate of the Ungodly

In the speeches of the dialogue section, apart from the disputational discourse on both sides, it is the arguments of the friends that stand over against the laments of Job. Dominating this argumentation is the theme of the fate of the ungodly (the transgressors, the fools, etc.), a theme which occurs in each of the friends' speeches in both the first and the second cycle of discourse. Indeed, in all these passages there is really only one statement which gets developed, altered, and expanded, namely, the statement that transgressors will perish. Looking at all six variations on this same theme, one can nonetheless recognize a deliberate structure and a definite arrangement of the individual motifs:

	Eliphaz	Bildad	Zophar
I	4:7–11	8:8–19	11:11
	5:2–7		(27:13–23)
II	15:17–35	18:5–21	20:4–25

In the first cycle of discourse, the fate of the ungodly is one argument alongside others. The argument is circumscribed about only one point: the end of the transgressor. This motif is neither expanded to include a look at the whole life of the transgressor nor employed as a justification for the fate of the transgressor.

The three presentations of this argument are characteristically differentiated in the three speeches. In the speech of Eliphaz the emphasis lies upon the fact of the transgressor's fate as such, as is shown both at the beginning in 4:7-9 and at the conclusion in 5:6-7. Only here at the beginning of the argument (4:7-9) is openly stated both the fact that and the reason why Job must be set straight: the innocent never perish (re: Job's asseveration of innocence), only the transgressors. This thesis is underlined by means of the image employed in vv. 10-11: the devouring lions (described in five different ways) are destroyed. Job 5:2 ties directly into 4:9-11 and repeats the thesis in different words. The demise of "the fool" is then elaborated upon from two sides in vv. 3-5. (1) The fool can indeed take root, but then all at once he perishes (v. 3). (2) Whatever of the fool's that might survive his immediate demise is ultimately dragged down to ruin with him, such as his house, his children, or his possessions (vv. 3b-5).

The expansion in the first direction listed above is further developed in Bildad's speech in 8:8-19. The notion that the transgressor can take root but then suddenly perishes is here amplified by means of two sets of plant imagery (vv. 11-14, 15-18) whereby the plants in question sprout luxuriously but then all at once wither and fade away.

The expansion in the second direction listed above gets developed in the speech of Zophar.[1] This speech deals chiefly with those things of the transgressor which might be left after his death: his children (27:14-15), his possessions (27:16-19), his house (27:18). At the same time, the central motif of the end of the transgressor is varyingly taken up in Bildad's speech in 8:19 and in Zophar's speech in 27:20-23 (here emphasizing the terrifying nature of that end). The conscious, systematic structure of the three speeches can also be seen in the way the argumentation is bolstered in each of the speeches. What is more, this is done with obviously deliberate intensification. Eliphaz refers to his own experience (4:9 and 5:3), Bildad recalls ancestral tradition (8:8-10),[2] and Zophar expresses the wish that God himself might speak to Job and reveal wisdom to him (11:5-6).

In all three speeches in the second cycle of discourse, the sole argument, alongside the disputational discourse, is the argument about the fate of the transgressor. This argument is elaborately developed, accompanied each time by a specific introduction and conclusion.[3] Hence this argument is most emphatically character- ized as being quite simply the decisive argument of the friends. Moreover, this motif of the end of the transgressor is here devel- oped along two fronts: (1) Not only the end but indeed the whole life of the transgressor is held in view ("The wicked man writhes in pain all his days" [15:20]). (2) In all three speeches (only intimated in the second), a reason is given for the fate of the transgressor. According to Eliphaz, the transgressor has rebelled against God (15:25–28); according to Bildad, he has set obstacles in the way of the righteous (implied in 18:7–8); and according to Zophar, he has plundered the livelihood of the poor (20:19–21).[4]

In this way our three passages from the second cycle of discourse attain a greater diversity than their counterparts in the first cycle. A deliberate sort of classifying within the three speeches can be recog- nized in the way that the three major boons to life, the gifts which are able to outlast death, are each emphasized in turn in one of the three speeches of the second cycle of discourse. Eliphaz talks about the fruits of life, including the blessing of children (15:29–33); the existence of the transgressor is without fruit, as is stated once again at the conclusion of Eliphaz's speech (15:34–35). Bildad directs at- tention to the place of habitation (18:5–6, 14–15, 18, 21); in his concluding remark he expressly states, "Surely such are the dwell- ings of the ungodly" (18:21). Possessions are the theme of Zophar's speech (20:12–18, 22–23, 28). Common to all three speeches is the claim that the transgressor is haunted by anxiety all his days (15:20–24; 18:7–10, 11–22; 20:24–27). In addition, all three speeches contain a series of images further depicting the fate of the transgressor.

What is the origin of this argument about the fate of the un- godly? Certainly the argument grows out of a person's own experi- ence, but it has also been handed down as folk wisdom; indeed, the argument can even be claimed to rest upon divine revelation (see above). But how and where has this argument been transmitted? At first glance we recognize a broad stream of tradition which has served to mediate this argument about the fate of the ungodly, namely, the wisdom tradition of Israel, reflected in Proverbs. In- deed, Proverbs offers a whole array of parallels to the statement that the ungodly will perish (e.g., Prov. 12:7–21). When experience is referred to as the source of this argument, as in Job 4:8, that is most in keeping with the spirit of the wisdom tradition. The admonition to Job that he take to heart what is being said to him is also typical of wisdom speech. Hence there can be no doubt that the friends speak the language of wisdom in advancing this argument about the fate of the ungodly.

However, if one looks closely one sees at least one point at which the speech of the friends is clearly to be distinguished from the language of Proverbs. This point has to do with the fate of the ungodly. The flat, even juxtaposition of the righteous and the ungodly in one sentence, as occurs persistently in Proverbs, occurs not a single time in the speeches of Job's friends! Nowhere in the speeches of the friends do we find a sentence corresponding, for example, to "No ill befalls the righteous, but the wicked are filled with trouble" (Prov. 12:21). There is here a second and even more important determination: in the speeches of the friends, talk about the fate of the righteous is part of a different form of speech than talk about the fate of the ungodly. This fact has already been demonstrated from one perspective. The passages just treated which deal with the argument of the fate of the ungodly exhibit not a single case of direct paralleling with the fate of the righteous, nor do these passages anywhere display any transition from the one argument to the other. The motif of the fate of the righteous is nowhere to be found in the whole second cycle of discourse. We will demonstrate later that this motif about the fate of the righteous is actually independent of its counterpart and part of a totally different form of speech.

The upshot of all this is that it is inaccurate to derive the talk about the fate of the ungodly in the speeches of the friends directly from the corresponding forms of speech in the wisdom material. Rather, from the standpoint of the history of traditions, we clearly see here two stages of development. Furthermore, it is a priori more probable to regard as the later stage that stage where the full and even paralleling of the fates of the ungodly and the pious is carried out. Now the question arises as to whether we can still recognize a course of tradition which has an earlier stage reflected in the speeches of the friends, where they talk about the fate of the transgressor, and a later stage reflected in Proverbs. For the most part, it is in the individual lament psalms that we find speech about the transgressors, their actions, and also the consequences of those actions. More precisely, we are talking here about one subcategory of the lament, namely, the lament about enemies. The designations of these "transgressors," "fools," "wicked," and so forth in the speeches of the friends occur almost without exception in Psalms as ways of identifying the opponents of the lamenter. I have attempted elsewhere to sketch the development of this component of the lament.[5] The lament about enemies first of all directs attention to an *act* of the enemy (or transgressor, etc.).[6] In most cases, this act is an attack upon the lamenter. Psalms speaks of this attack in three broad groups of images:

1. The enemies set nets or traps (e.g., Ps. 140:4b–5[5b–6]).
2. The enemies are compared to wild animals who fall upon the lamenter (e.g., Ps. 22:12–13, 16[13–14, 17]).
3. The enemies are attacking warriors or plaintiffs in a lawsuit (e.g., Ps. 7:12[13]).[7]

Two of these groups of images occur with a noticeable concentration of terminology where the motif of the fate of the transgressor appears in the speeches of the friends: right at the beginning of the first speech of Eliphaz, just after the introduction in 4:10–11, and then in the second speech of Bildad, at 18:7–10. In the first of these passages, in the repeatedly varied clauses about the destruction of the devouring lions, five terms for "lion" are used; in the second passage five terms are used to describe the traps and snares in which the transgressor, after he has set them up, is himself caught. There can be no doubt at all that both the traditional groups of images so richly attested in Psalms are here deliberately used to describe the actions of the transgressors. It is apparent already from the structure of chap. 4 that the image in vv. 10–11 is placed next to the determination in vv. 8–9 without any sort of connective word. This fact is most easily explained if the association of the image with the statement about the transgressors' being doomed to destruction was already given in the tradition. This same association can be seen in Ps. 58:6[7]: "O God, break the teeth in their mouths; tear out the fangs of the young lions, O Lord!" The Hebrew words for "roar" (*š'g*) and "prey" (*ṭrp*) from Job 4:10–11 both occur in Ps. 22:13[14]; both the noun and the verb of Job 4:10b are also found in Ps. 58:6[7].[8]

That the terminology dealing with the setting of traps in 18:7–10 has its original setting in the lament about enemies, as one type of individual lament psalm, needs no additional proof.[9] The five terms used here for net or trap occur almost exclusively in the lament about enemies within the individual lament psalms; each of the clauses in vv. 7b–10 has its parallel in those psalms.

However, both these groups of images from the individual lament psalms deal with only one aspect of the lament about enemies, namely, with the attack of the enemies (= transgressors) against the lamenter. This aspect naturally recedes totally into the background in the speeches of the friends, where the focus is upon the essence of the transgressors. In the laments found in Psalms, this latter focus of interest is recognizable as a development of the lament, which in keeping with its essence could originally refer only to the actions which affected the lamenter. The statements in Psalms about the essence of the transgressors fall into two groups: the transgressors are by nature wicked in their behavior (I) toward God and (II) toward their fellows.[10] Both occur in the second cycle of discourse and in the motivation clauses advanced by Bildad in 15:25–28 and Zophar in 20:19–21.[11] This description of the enemies in their essence is expanded through reflection upon their fate; even if they thrive for a long time, being rich and powerful, ultimately they will suffer a terrible end: ". . . until I went into the sanctuary of God; then I perceived their end" (Ps. 73:17). (Verses 18–20 go on to speak of this end, quite similar to the way in which this motif is handled in the speeches of the friends.)

Thus we have arrived at the motif which is developed in the speeches of the friends, namely, the motif of the end of the transgressor. Psalm 73 reveals particularly clearly how this motif has developed out of the lament; however, it is the history of the motif as a whole which confirms this pattern of development. To give another example, in Ps. 52:5[7] destruction at the hands of God is pronounced upon the transgressor.[12] Already within the history of the psalm of lamentation, the subcategory of the lament about enemies becomes so expanded that this particular type of utterance separates itself from the strict genre of the lament and becomes a substantiating, reflective speech *about* the transgressor. That this sort of utterance then becomes wisdom speech is in no way surprising; indeed, the substantiating of something on the basis of reflection is precisely characteristic of wisdom! And so, when already Psalm 73 has affinities to wisdom speech because of this fundamental characteristic of wisdom, then in Psalm 37 the transition from individual lamentation to wisdom speech is a simply brilliant maneuver. Psalm 37 exhibits a whole array of parallels to the speeches of the friends (above all, to chap. 20). It is thus confirmed that we are to see the origin of the friends' argument about the "fate of the transgressor" in an expansion of one category of the individual lament psalm, namely, the lament about enemies.[13] Thus there is not only a series of parallels in Psalms to the central motif of the "end of the transgressor,"[14] but there are also parallels for the development of this motif in terms of its particulars. All that might survive the death of the transgressor will perish with him: children (Ps. 109:9–10, 13a), possessions (Ps. 109:11), memory (Ps. 109:13b, 15b).

Job's Counterargument: Chapter 21

This chapter reveals the high artistry of the poet of Job in a very special way. In no other chapter does the person who has composed this drama step so closely to the fore. As happens so often, so also here the skill of the poet is shown in the sparing use of his material. In point of fact this counterspeech of Job—the only speech in which Job confronts his friends with arguments—contains only the very same motifs which go to make up the argument in the speeches of the friends. Through only minimal alterations, the same motifs are here transformed into their most blatant opposites. The motif of the end of the transgressor underlies vv. 17–33; vv. 7–13 speak of the good fortune of the transgressor, while vv. 14–15 speak of his godlessness (and v. 31 summarizes his remaining misdeeds). All these motifs occur in the speeches of the friends; outright parallels to most of the clauses in chap. 21 are to be found there. The only difference in chap. 21 is that Job takes what the friends maintain concerning the end of the transgressor and calls it into question, and where the friends seek to circumscribe the good fortune of the transgressor as much as possible, Job emphasizes it and elaborates upon it. Or looking at it from the standpoint of the psalms of lamentation (to which this speech of Job stands in closer proximity than do the arguments of the friends), Job turns into statement of fact that which the righteous bemoan concerning the ungodly in the psalms of lamentation (namely, that everything goes well for them despite their godlessness). Job calls into question what the righteous in the psalms of lamentation implore of God concerning the transgressors, or what they pronounce as certain. And to be sure, he does this simply on the basis of reality. Job says to the friends: your theories are not in accord with reality, reality differs from your theology. As the introduction in vv. 2–6 shows, Job is thoroughly aware of what he is saying here. What Job must now say is something terrifying, not only for the friends but also for him:

> Look at me, and be appalled,
> and lay your hand upon your mouth.
> When I think of it I am dismayed,
> and shuddering seizes my flesh. (21:5–6)

It is revolutionary for the piety of his time, whose fundamental tenets are here in danger of toppling. In all this Job goes only one small step beyond what the friends also say. The friends likewise speak of the good fortune of the ungodly, of their wealth, of their being blessed with progeny, and of the heights to which they attain. To be sure, they suppress as much as possible the fact that these things happen, but even they are unable to deny the facts. Sometimes these facts are more strongly emphasized in the psalms of lamentation.[15] Job takes only that one small additional step, in that these clauses are for him no longer laments but matters of fact, and he strongly emphasizes that this is so (21:7–13 and 16, taken up again in vv. 23, 24, 30, 32, 33). In contrast to Psalm 73, which opposes to the good fortune of the transgressors their ultimate demise and therein is freed from the burden of having to acknowledge the good fortune of the ungodly, Job questions precisely whether the end of the transgressor is always and necessarily a terrible one (vv. 17–33). Between the two chief parts of Job's speech stands a quotation from a transgressor (vv. 14–16); this quotation openly and unhesitatingly renounces God.[16] Both the chief parts begin with a question: why (v. 7) and how often (v. 17). Behind the why in v. 7 stands the accusation against God: Why does God allow it? However, the question is here directed to the friends and is intended to be a substantive inquiry into the motivation behind God's actions.[17] In the course of the broad description of the good fortune of the transgressors, the three blessings constitutive of good fortune which we know from the arguments of the friends appear once again: progeny (v. 8), home (v. 9), and possessions (v. 10). Added to these are health and long life (v. 7), the charming picture of the mirth of children (vv. 11–12), and a quick and easy death (v. 13). This description has something uncanny about it. In itself it says nothing other than what the friends must also admit, namely, that there are ungodly who live lives of good fortune. But the uncanny element comes in through the extensive depiction of this good fortune; all this could just as well be a description of someone blessed by God! In effect, however, this quite simply means a terrifying breach in the old, established faith (hence the introduction in vv. 5–6). Job sees and openly states that in the world there is such a thing as blessedness without blessing, divine favor without God, salvation without a savior! The ancient equation between blessing and good fortune, which is fundamental to the Old Testament, is shattered for Job. Now Job addresses himself to the objection which the friends raise at this point (e.g., in 18:5 or 20:6), namely, that even if there is such a thing as good fortune for the ungodly, this good fortune carries with it a terrifying end. Job asks how often this is really so, and he answers that the reality of the situation appears otherwise. All are united in death, whether death be timely or ill-fated (cf. 3:11–20); in other words, both kinds of death are to be found among both the righteous and the ungodly (vv. 23–26). Catastrophes often bypass the transgressor (vv. 27–30); he dies a peaceful death, honored by all (vv. 32–33), with no one having dared to hold up his deeds against him (v. 31). Earlier Job had brushed aside the objection that, when a transgressor dies in peace, punishment devolves upon the children; now Job goes on to say that if there is such a thing as retribution it must affect the transgressor himself or else it has no meaning (vv. 19–21[18]). The sort of wisdom tirelessly proclaimed in Proverbs, namely, that things will go well for the righteous and *must* go ill for the transgressor, is here challenged on every score. From the standpoint of the friends this is nothing other than blasphemy; the fundamentals of their theology would collapse under such views. With this final speech, in which Job maintains that a transgressor who has denied God (vv. 14–15) can still live in good fortune (vv. 7–16) and die in peace (vv. 17–33), Job has so provoked his friends that now from their side a final and conclusive statement simply *must* be made. This comes in the speech of Eliphaz (chap. 22), who now pronounces the unveiled accusation: Job *is* a transgressor. Now the discussion is at an end; hereafter it is no longer possible. In his speech in chap. 22 Eliphaz no longer enters at all into the—for him—terrible things which Job has said in chap. 21, but instead he simply goes over to direct accusation. Similarly, in chap. 23 Job maintains his silence in face of the accusation of Eliphaz and now turns toward God alone.[19]

The Good Fortune of the Righteous

This motif is not the corresponding parallel to the above-mentioned "fate of the transgressor." Nowhere in the Book of Job do we find *in one and the same sentence* the juxtaposition of the respective fates of the righteous and the ungodly such as we encounter so frequently in Proverbs. And yet, the beatification or promise of salvation directed to the righteous is an element often found in Proverbs.[20] In several places the prerequisite for such beatification is the readiness to accept discipline.[21] All these passages point in the direction of a fixed form, a properly cultic form which on the basis of Psalm 91 is best designated as an assurance of blessing [*Segenszusage*]. This form is reflected in Deut. 28:3–6 and 30:5–9; Psalm 128 is also such an assurance of blessing. Thus this motif has an origin quite different from that of the motif of the "fate of the transgressor."

Regarding the distribution of the motif of the good fortune of the righteous, the following picture emerges: It is contained in all three of the friends' speeches in the first cycle of discourse, it is totally absent in the second cycle, and in the third cycle it returns once again in the speech of Eliphaz. The four passages in question (5:8, 17, 21–26; 8:5–7, 21–22; 11:13–20; 22:21–30) share a corresponding structure but also display characteristic differences. The three latter passages are cast in a conditional mode: "if you . . . then. . . ." The first speech, by Eliphaz, appears to be an unconditioned promise of salvation; according to its form, this speech is not a conditional statement. In reality, however, the promise *is* conditioned; it is just that the condition is very cautiously formulated and deliberately separated from the element of promise.[22] That corresponds to the overall mood of this first of the friends' speeches. The condition is consistently the same in the other three passages, being either (a) if you return to God[23] or (b) if you put aside your sins.[24] All three passages also have the same conclusion, namely, the double promise (or promise directed along two avenues), which corresponds to the double wish so frequently found at the end of the psalms of lamentation. It is striking here how the misfortune pictured in 5:21-22 is held out as a prospect for the opponents of Job, how the same happens with regard to the transgressors in 11:18-20, and how in 22:29-30 the humble and the transgressor are impersonally juxtaposed to each other. All these clauses sound so stereotyped, all are so similar to one another, that there must be a quite definite cultic rite somewhere close at hand. Fixed components of this rite must have included a turning toward God accompanied by some act of renunciation, upon which will have followed a "lifting up of the head" (11:15; 22:26) and a recitation by friends of an assurance of salvation (or of blessing). Therefore the friends are directing Job toward a quite definite portal which he knows well. They are saying, "Job, you must pass through this portal; beyond this portal all good fortune awaits you."[25]

No One Righteous before God

This motif is stated in the first and second speeches of Eliphaz in 4:12-21 and 15:14-16, in the fragment which we have ascribed to Bildad in 25:4-6, and in Job's answer to the first speech of Bildad in 9:2. If the fragment 25:4-6 had its original setting at the conclusion of the first speech of Bildad, as we have demonstrated elsewhere,[26] then in 9:2 Job would be referring (with almost word-for-word correspondence) to a sentence that has just been spoken by Bildad. Thus the natural context of Job's speech is restored without difficulty. Our supposition regarding the fragment 25:4-6 receives additional support through the investigation of the motif at hand throughout the whole Book of Job. In all three places where this motif occurs in the speeches of the friends, it consists of a single sentence which each time is bolstered by a conclusion based on the logical principle of *a maiore ad minus*.[27] In this argument as found in chaps. 4 and 25, mankind is depicted in his frailty and lowliness over against the angels (4:18) and the stars (25:5). In 15:16, on the other hand, mankind is described in terms of his corruption and wickedness (also in contrast to the angels). This latter sort of comparison is certainly to be understood as an intensification. In his first speech Eliphaz wants to urge upon Job that simply as a mortal creature he cannot be in the right over against God; in his second speech, he emphasizes his point by speaking of human depravity. This is in accord with the intensifying line of thought in the speeches of the friends, leading up to the final accusation. In his third speech, in the place of this argument about the impossibility of being righteous before God, Eliphaz passes over to direct accusation; he openly accuses Job of just such depravity. It is not very likely, then, that this argument in its more modest form would crop up once again in chap. 25, in a third speech of Bildad, after its ultimate intensification in Eliphaz's accusation. Conversely, 25:4–6 fits very nicely into the first cycle of discourse, parallel to the initial wording of our argument in 4:17–21. All this is additional evidence for seeing 25:4–6 as originally belonging to the first speech of Bildad.

What is the origin of this motif, which appears in almost the same form in all three passages? In contrast to the other two motifs treated in this chapter, this one appears in a single sentence that is restricted in scope and narrowly defined in terms of its meaning This is the only argument of the friends to which Job gives assent, and thereby it receives a special importance. Job says, "Truly I know that it is so!" (9:2 = 25:4). The same sentence occurs in one of the psalms:[28]

> Enter not into judgment with thy servant;
> for no man living is righteous before thee. (Ps. 143:2)

Here in the psalm this argument is appended to a petition. Its function is clearly recognizable; it is to motivate God to intervene.[29] Substantively speaking, this is the same motivating argument that appears in Ps. 130:3 and that Luther correctly renders as "No one can boast of himself before you." The sentence in question has the same function as the allusion to the frailty of mankind which, for its own part, has considerable significance in the speeches of Job—

where it is also consistently associated with a petition or a wish. The supplicant seeks protection in the face of God's punishing interventon by referring to the fact that before the majesty of the judging God every person exhibits some sort of flaw. Perhaps the judge will be inclined toward greater leniency if he acknowledges this fact as a mitigating circumstance. But wherein is this assertion based? The sentence is quite simply grounded in the overall understanding within Israel of the divine-human relationship. This is most clearly expressed in Israel's praise of God.[30] Thus also in Job's answer this sentence naturally passes over into praise of God (9:3-12). However, it is also apparent here (esp. in 9:14-16, 32-33) that this sentence has a totally different meaning when voiced by the friends than it does when found in the mouth of Job. The sentence loses its meaning and its power to the degree that it is torn away from its proper function as a motif accompanying petition or as an indirect element of the praise of God and is made into an independent argument. The sentence, true in and of itself, no longer functions in its proper capacity. For Job, this sentence amounts only to a deepening of his despair; as a "general principle" it only makes his own fate all the more senseless and unbearable. Here the theological stance of the poet of Job is perhaps at its clearest: He stands over against a tendency thus to abstract theological statements out of their concrete setting in the situation of mankind before God, a tendency which then thinks it can use such abstracted and eternally valid sentences to dispose of matters concerning the nature of God and his activity. To this tendency our poet speaks a radical No. This sentence, transformed into an argument, namely, that no person is righteous before God, is as such a worthless argument precisely *because* both parties in the discourse assent to it. If the argument is true in this way, then it is too true to be of any use.

NOTES

1. With regard to the speech of Zophar in chap. 11, it is striking that the first part is elaborately introduced but that the part so introduced consists of only a single sentence (v. 11; perhaps v. 6c belongs here as well). This is hardly imaginable! The result is that the emphasis falls totally on vv. 13-19, which hold out the prospect of good fortune for Job. This corresponds very poorly to the pointed and hostile introduction in vv. 2-4. The section made up of vv. 13-19 has no real counterpart in the present text. In

light of the introduction and the parallels with the other speeches of the friends, such a counterpart could consist only in Zophar's also holding up to Job the picture of the fate of the ungodly. Only so would this speech come into equilibrium with both the preceding speeches of the friends. Such a passage as we are looking for appears in the Book of Job as a fragment, in 27:13-23. Job 27:13 could very well follow directly upon 11:11. Then this speech would be a precise parallel to both the corresponding parts in the speeches of Eliphaz and Bildad. Job 27:13-23 is a development of the theme of "the end of the transgressor." Verse 13 states the theme; vv. 14-15 deal with the progeny of the transgressor, vv. 16-19 with his possessions; vv. 20-22 state that the transgressor is seized by the powers of destruction (substantively corresponding to v. 13); and v. 23 shows the transgressor in disgrace.

2. Both these motifs are once again taken up by Eliphaz in the first speech of the second cycle of discourse.

3. Cf. Ps. 52:7[9], where such a conclusion also stands at the end of this motif.

4. The two reasons Eliphaz and Zophar give are employed in the third cycle of discourse (in chap. 22) as accusations against Job!

5. Claus Westermann, "Struktur und Geschichte der Klage im Alten Testament," *Zeitschrift für die alttestamentliche Wissenschaft* 66 (1954): 61-66.

6. Ibid., p. 62.

7. Ibid.; cf. here the lament about enemies in the laments of Job, pp. 43-46, above.

8. In Job 4:10b read *nittāṣû* in place of *nittā'û,* following the critical apparatus of Rudolf Kittel, ed., *Biblia Hebraica,* 3d ed. (Stuttgart, 1937); cf. also Ps. 7:2[3]; 17:12; 35:16-17.

9. Cf. the passages listed in Hermann Gunkel and Joachim Begrich, *Einleitung in die Psalmen* (Göttingen, 1933), p. 198; the relevant passages from the Book of Job are not listed there, however.

10. On I cf. Ps. 14:1, 3-4 (= 53:1, 3-4); 26:10; 28:4; 36:4[5]; 52:1[3]; 55:10-11, 15[11-12, 16]; 73:6; 109:17. On II cf. Ps. 5:10[11]; 10:3; 14:1; 28:5; 36:1[2]; 52:7[9]; 54:3[5]; 55:19[20]; 73:23; 86:14; 119:85, 139. Cf. also Westermann, "Struktur," p. 63, nn. 4, 5.

11. Here also one can adduce direct parallels; on Job 15:25-28 cf. Ps. 139:20-21 and 5:10[11]; on Job 15:27 along with v. 25 cf. Ps. 73:3 along with v. 9! On Job 20:19-21 cf. Ps. 94:5-6; 10:8; 37:14 (cf. Ps. 37:15 with Job 20:25); 109:16.

12. With a series of verbs which also occur where this motif is treated in the Book of Job.

13. Cf. Westermann, "Struktur," p. 64.

14. On the "end of the transgressor" cf. Ps. 11:6; 14:5; 21:8-10[9-11]; 37:20; 49:10-20[11-21]; 53:5[6]; 63:9-10[10-11]; 64:7-8[8-9]; 73:17-20; 75:8[9]; 92:7[8].

15. Cf., e.g., Ps. 73:3-9, 12 or 10:5-6; cf. also Ps. 17:14b; 49:6[7]; 52:7b[9b].

16. Cf. n. 11 above and the obvious parallels in Ps. 73:9, 11; cf. also Ps. 10:3b-4, 11; 14:1, 4c; 28:5; 36:1[2]; 54:3b[5b]; 86:14. When here in chap. 21 the two motifs of the godlessness of the transgressor and the good fortune of the transgressor stand juxtaposed as they do in Psalms 10, 54, or 73, this fact alone seems to me to offer a sure confirmation for the thesis that the motifs of the individual lament psalm are presupposed in Job 21.

17. Hence the use of מדוע instead of למה as the "why"!

18. Verse 22 is the gloss of some dismayed scribe.

19. Apparently the fragment composed of 23:15 and 24:1-4, 9, 21-25 (except for v. 24) was intended for this speech of Job in chap. 21. The actions of the transgressors are described, and this leads to the question of why God does not judge the transgressor. In connection with chap. 21, this fragment is both intelligible and a logical expansion.

20. Cf. Prov. 16:20; 22:4; 28:14; cf. also Ps. 34:8b[9b].

21. Cf. Prov. 10:17a; 13:18b; 15:32. A closer parallel to Job 5:21-26 is offered by Psalm 91; in addition, on v. 26 cf. Ps. 92:14[15]; on v. 21 cf. Ps. 31:20[21]; on v. 19 cf. Ps. 37:19 and 34:20[21].

22. The conditional element of 5:8, which is taken up again in v. 17, is separated from the promise of salvation in vv. 21-26 by the praise of the protecting God in vv. 18-20.

23. Cf. Job 8:5; 11:13; 22:23; cf. the element of the "turning toward God," which has its place in the psalms of lamentation between the lament and the petition: Ps. 44:20[21]; 88:9[10]; 143:6; Exod. 9:29; Ezra 9:5.

24. Job 8:6a; 11:14; 22:23b (the element of renunciation).

25. The cultic overtones are very obvious in 22:25-28: the one who is crying out in his distress finds a hearing (v. 27a); now he can pay the vows made while in distress (v. 27b); now he can lift up his head as the one who has been blessed and can rejoice in God his Savior (cf. Ps. 32:7, 11).

26. See above, p. 77.

27. On 4:17 cf. vv. 18-21; on 15:14 cf. vv. 15-16; on 25:4 cf. vv. 5-6; cf. also 9:2.

28. Cf. 1 Kings 8:46; Eccles. 7:21 [sic, cf. v. 20]; Prov. 10:9 [sic].

29. By the way, note also the motif of human frailty in v. 7aβ and v. 7bβ.

30. Cf. Ps. 76:7b[8b]; 89:8[9]; 113:5; 36:6[7]; 111:3, 7; 33:4-5; 100:3; 148:13b; 1 Sam. 2:2.

7

The Asseveration of Innocence

The asseveration of innocence [*Unschuldsbeteuerung*] is a fixed form in the psalms of lamentation.[1] Under certain circumstances it can there take the place of the confession of sins. The friends demand of Job such a confession, but Job counters with his asseveration of innocence. This occurs in two acts. In the first, Job faces up to his friends and maintains his innocence. In 6:28–30 this asseveration stands totally within the context of the disputational discourse. Job attempts to convince his friends that he is not the transgressor his friends suspect him of being (despite God's blows against him). This attempt echoes once again in Job's fifth speech, which is to say in the last speech where there is disputational discourse between Job and the friends ("Know then that God has put me in the wrong!" [19:6]). However, none of this is actually asseveration of innocence; it is only a reflection of it. Already in his second speech Job turns to the higher court with an asseveration of innocence. And just as his lament at the beginning is no more than a cry (chap. 3), so here is the affirmation of his innocence no more than a single very short statement voiced to God: "I am blameless" (9:21).[2] But just a little further on this sentence gets transposed into its opposite: "I must indeed be guilty" (9:29).[3] The same thing occurs once again at 10:6, in the same speech. All these clauses from the second speech of Job stand in very close association with the accusation against God. The asseveration of innocence arises out of this other element, initially as the cry of one who has become conscious of his total alienation and despair. By the time of the third speech, however, the situation is different. Here a conclusion gets drawn out of the despairing cry:

Behold, he will slay me; I have no hope;
yet will I defend my ways to his face. (13:15; cf. vv. 18, 23)

What it comes down to is that already here, at the end of the first cycle of discourse, the resolve is formed which then gets carried out in chap. 31. In the second cycle of discourse, correspondingly, the asseveration of innocence does not appear as an independent form. The closest thing to it in this cycle is found in 16:17, which shows that Job still stands by his earlier asseveration.[4] The asseveration of innocence reappears in the third cycle of discourse, in Job's answer to the final speech of Eliphaz. Tying in directly and almost word-for-word with 13:5, it occurs in 23:7, 10, 12. In these verses the asseveration of innocence is firmly allied with the wish to stand in the presence of God, where one would be able to present one's case to him (23:2-6). The final speech of Job contains only these two motifs, followed by the accusation against God in 23:13-17. If one ignores for the moment the fragments in chaps. 24-27, then the final speech of Job is followed, after the intervening section comprised of chap. 28, by the large concluding lament in chaps. 29-31. Within the fragments, the element of asseveration of innocence occurs only in 27:2-6. These verses have the character of a solemn new point of emphasis, one can even say of an actual introduction. However, the theme here finds no continuation; various fragments follow in 27:7ff. It has often been noted, on the other hand, how remarkably abruptly the oath of clearance starts out in chap. 31. Houtsma, among others, has suspected that the beginning of chap. 31 is to be found in 27:2-6.[5] This is certainly the case. We can here add two more relevant arguments: (1) In 23:7, 10-12 the asseveration of innocence is conjoined with the accusation against God; the one passes over into the other. The final and definitive appearance of the element of asseveration of innocence in chap. 31 then follows upon the element of accusation. (2) We saw that the asseveration of innocence encompassed two acts: over against the friends— over against God. Now Job, who since the utterance of Eliphaz in chap. 22 had no longer addressed the friends, turns to them one more time right at the end; 27:5 is Job's only rebuttal of the accusation of Eliphaz in chap. 22. From now on, however, with his oath of clearance, Job has nothing more to do with the friends; from here on he deals only with God. All this is not really apparent when one reads 27:2–6 in its present position, but it is readily apparent if these words introduce the concluding speech of Job, namely, his oath of clearance in chap. 31.

It was shown above that the asseveration of innocence, where it occurs in the speeches of Job, corresponds to the asseveration of innocence as found in the psalms of lamentation. Job's oath of clearance in chap. 31 is no more than a development of the same process, which therefore certainly has a cultic background.[6]

Chapter 31 contains only two themes: asseveration of innocence (vv. 1–34, 38–40) and wish (vv. 35–37). The conclusion, vv. 35–37, is certainly a summoning of God in terms of its content; in terms of its form, however, it remains a wish. Here we find a precise correspondence to the beginning of chap. 23, which is the final speech of Job: it begins with the same wish (vv. 2–6), which then passes over into the asseveration of innocence (vv. 7, 10–12). Hence the situation looks like this:

Beginning (chap. 23): The wish to stand before God, together with an asseveration of innocence;

End (chap. 31): An asseveration of innocence, together with the wish to stand before God.

NOTES

1. Cf. Hermann Gunkel and Joachim Begrich, *Einleitung in die Psalmen* (Göttingen, 1933), p. 253.

2. The expression *tom 'ānî* most likely stems from juristic speech.

3. [Westermann's reading of the text's ארשע אנכי differs slightly from the RSV at this point.—Trans.]

4. On 19:6 see above.

5. Martijn Theodoor Houtsma, *Das Buch Hiob,* Textkritische Studien zum Alten Testament 1 (Leiden, 1925), p. 61.

6. On the religiohistorical background of this "negative confession," cf. Paul Humbert, *Recherches sur les sources égyptiennes de la littérature sapientale d'Israel,* Mémoires de l'Université de Neuchâtel 7 (Neuchâtel, 1929); cf. also Curt Kuhl, "Neuere Literarkritik des Buches Hiob," *Theologische Rundschau,* N.F. 21 (1953): 293.

8

The Avowal of Trust

The avowal of trust [*Bekenntnis der Zuversicht*] occurs only in 16:19-21 and 19:25-27. These passages are in the first and second speeches of the second cycle of discourse, which are the same two speeches in which the accusation against God assumes the form of the lament about enemies. Both these trustful utterances therefore stand over against the sharpest form of accusation against God in their same respective speeches. In chap. 16 the avowal is allied with a cry of despair ("O earth, cover not my blood!"), the cry of an innocent man who foresees a violent death without any prospect of being rescued. All that is now left for him is the court of justice which disposes of his case. God is the real focus of attention in this cry, but just as in chap. 3 so also here, in a situation of extreme distress, the language reverts to primitive patterns. What Job foresees is the concrete, bitter reality of his death, complete with the exposure of his corpse and the spilling of his blood. It would be the final straw for his blood to vanish into the earth. However, it is just this which cannot be; the earth is not allowed quietly to swallow it up! The blood cries from the earth (Genesis 4). But who other than God can hear it? Thus it is precisely this archaic, primitive conception which leads to the paradoxical situation of calling upon God for protection against God:

> . . . My eye pours out tears to God,
> that he would maintain the right of a man [in dispute] with God
> and between a man and his neighbor.[1] (16:20b-21)

This is the context in which the avowal of trust occurs here:

> Even now, behold, my witness is in heaven,
> and he that vouches for me is on high! (16:19)

Job's situation is depicted in terms of a legal proceeding. The judge (God) has already—or so it seems—decided against Job (even though he is innocent; 16:19). But Job cannot acquiesce in the judgment. There must still be one who will intervene for him against the verdict. But that one can be, once again, only God! We have here an avowal of trust at the most extreme limits, a reliance upon God against God. It is already apparent here why the genre of the avowal of trust occurs so rarely in the speeches of Job: silently contained within this genre is a polemic against any trust in God that has become too cheap, stereotyped, and inauthentic. It is precisely such a trust in God that is no longer possible for Job. For Job, trust in God has become a risk undertaken at the outer limits.

The avowal of trust in 19:25–27 stands in a similar context. The wish in 19:23–24 is a precise formal correspondence to that in 16:18; this wish is allied with an expression of certainty, here more forcibly and expansively stated than in chap. 16 but otherwise essentially the same. Job 19:25 is substantially the same as 16:19. The text immediately following v. 25 is disrupted and cannot yet be reconstructed with certainty; only the final clauses of vv. 26 and 27 are still clear: ". . . I shall see God . . . and my eyes shall behold the one no longer foreign to me." The whole discussion about whether or not Job here expresses hope in resurrection bypasses the sense of the text. Job can do no more than place himself on the side of God, over against God. That much has already been said in 16:18–21; nothing more than this is said in chap. 19. Job 19:23–27 goes beyond chap. 16 only insofar as Job here develops in a little more detail his extreme possibility. But just what does it mean in this case when Job, certain of his impending death, *nevertheless* continues to trust in God? It can only mean that, despite his sentence of death, he still expects legal assistance from God against God (16:19; 19:25). Despite his death, he still expects legal intervention *against* his death, which is to say "after" his death. The intent behind this pattern of development is simply to strengthen Job's certainty. Job says, in effect, "I cling to the hope that the impossible will happen." It is a complete misunderstanding so to generalize the expressions here that they become a "presentiment" of resurrection or of life after death. The emphasis does not lie upon *how* it will be possible for Job to receive justice from God despite his having to die; the point is only *that* it will happen. To the extent to which these clauses here are detached from Job's concrete situation and made into generalized expressions, they are necessarily distorted.[2]

NOTES

1. The three components of the lament are clearly displayed in this utterance.

2. The comments upon these verses are endless; cf. Curt Kuhl, "Neuere Literarkritik des Buches Hiob," *Theologische Rundschau,* N.F. 21 (1953): 273–75. This whole discussion is worthless because it tears several clauses out of their context and approaches them from the perspective of a question which lies far removed from that context. A thorough treatment of this passage would have to (1) pay attention to the role of this form of speech (the avowal of trust) in the structure of the speeches of Job as a whole and (2) view this passage against the background of the proper history of this form of speech, which is to say study the avowal of trust as it appears in Psalms.

9

The Speeches of God

Considered from the standpoint of its form, God's answer is a disputation speech. It is expressly introduced as such (38:2-3 = 40:1, 2, 6, 7). Although expanded and varied in many ways, it is couched as a grand question to Job ("I will question you, and you shall declare to me!" [38:3b]), and a question it remains to the very end. Even the imperatives which occur are meant as interrogatives. For example, "Deck yourself with majesty and dignity" (40:10a) says in effect, "Are you perchance adorned with . . . ?" In this disputation form, the speeches of God tie in with the whole of the Book of Job (cf. the schema above, p. 4). All the participants in the drama—the friends, Job, and God—employ this disputation form. Job's final lament ends with the summoning of God to a lawsuit (31:35-37). However, this summons is couched in the wish that God would at least answer him. Certainly it is no human being whom he summons to a lawsuit! This wish, to which the whole course of the drama leads, is fulfilled for Job. God answers him (38:1; 40:1, 6). To be sure, this answer does not correspond to what Job had expected. In this answer Job neither learns the indictment against him (31:35)—and thereby the reason for God's terrible anger against him—nor finds either the advocate or the vindication for which, despite all appearances to the contrary, he had been waiting (16:19-21; 19:25). But none of that alters the basic fact that God does answer him. One could almost say that the *fact* of God's answering gets overlooked in the consideration of *what* God says.

The full significance of God's answering Job becomes apparent only when viewed against the background of the book's structure. We have seen how the element of a summons to a lawsuit is contained in the wish that God might answer Job. Here converge two lines that have run through the whole book so far: the legal proceeding and the lament. In line with the legal proceeding, Job, who was accused by the friends of being a transgressor (chap. 22), appeals to that higher court which is at the same time, however, the very opponent he summons to a lawsuit. In line with the lament, that point is now reached at which, in the genre of the lament psalm, the answer of God is expected. This is the point at which, in several communal lament psalms, God's answer is rendered directly (e.g., Ps. 85:8), and in several individual lament psalms God's favorable response is indicated by a singular hiatus (e.g., Ps. 28:6ff. after vv. 1–5). Begrich has shown how the cultic tradition of the "salvation oracle" [*Heilsorakel*] stands behind this phenomenon. This is the background against which the fact of God's answering Job is to be understood. God's answer comes at that point where, in the psalms of lamentation, there occurs the divine response to the pleading to God out of deep distress.

With the first element of God's speech being a rebuke (38:2; 40:2, 8), Job is here reproved for one of the strands in his discourse, namely, that line in which he thinks he can talk to God on an equal footing, summon him to a lawsuit, confront him as a legal opponent ("Will you condemn me that you may be justified?" [40:8b]). When he hears this rebuke, Job submits (40:4–5). But this is not the whole story; the other strand remains subtly in control: God has spoken to Job; Job's yearning for an answer to his deeply distressed pleading has been satisfied. According to the theology of the friends, God should have responded by shattering Job, thereby executing upon Job the punishment which they were sure had already been determined for him (even Job reckoned with the possibility of such a response [13:14–16]). But that is *not* how God responds. God *speaks,* and this *speaking* is the goodness, the assurance, the mercy [*ḥsd*] of God which comes to Job. This is what Job acknowledges in his response at 42:5.

In Psalms, retrospection upon the distress out of which God has saved the petitioner always contains two themes:

He inclined to me and heard my cry. (Ps. 40:2b)

He drew me up from the desolate pit. (Ps. 40:3a)

Job 42:5 corresponds to the first theme: Job acknowledges that God has encountered him. The other theme is intentionally excluded from the Job-drama proper. With God's speaking to Job the drama is concluded. Nothing more needs to be said, for that says it all. Nonetheless, the second theme, the "drawing out of the pit," finds its corresponding expression in the concluding portion of the narrative framework ("And the Lord restored the fortunes of Job" [42:10]).

What then is the meaning of God's answer as formulated? The One challenged by Job speaks as the Challenger. As such he puts *one* question to Job: Who are you? (38:2). This question sets up an unqualified alternative: Are you Creator or creature? Are you God or man? The question therefore has the character of a reproof (see above, p. 21). This becomes particularly obvious in 40:9–14: In his speech Job had overestimated himself. If he were able to answer God's question in the affirmative, God would recognize him as the creator and the lord of history (40:14). But what actually happens here is that God pushes Job to the spot where Job must acknowledge *God* to be Creator and Lord—which is also the *only* spot where Job can experience and receive the assurance of God, the intervention of God *on his behalf* (40:14b is actually descriptive praise).

The extent to which this question is developed (from 38:1 to 41:34) cannot conceal the fact that it is only *one* question. In asking him "Are you the creator?" God sets Job to rights. But why the extensive elaboration? We do not yet know for sure. However, if one detaches this whole piece from its form of querying reproof and at the same time transposes it from direct to indirect discourse, then it reveals itself for what it really is: a powerfully developed praise of God the creator. Even in the form which it has taken in the Book of Job, it is indirectly praise of the creator. The structure of this large complex will then best be understood on the basis of comparison with the corresponding motif in Psalms, namely, the "praise of the creator." Along with disputation, praise of the creator is a motif which ties together all three characters in the drama. We found it in the friends and in Job. In both cases, however, it suffered peculiar distortion. With Job, especially in chaps. 9–10, the motif is uncannily close to an indictment; with the friends, it appears more like praise of a principle. In both cases the praise of God is colored by the respective views of God; neither utters unencumbered praise of the sovereign God. But that is the thrust of what is said in the speeches of God: unencumbered praise of the sovereign God, liberation of the praise of God from the world-views of Job and his friends. The Accuser (1:9) had asked, "Does Job fear God *for nought*?" expecting (2:5) that "in truth, he will curse you to your face!" What finally remains is the unqualified alternative: bless (praise) God or curse him. The question is whether Job will stand by his original affirmation (1:21); the resolution occurs at the end, where Job bows before God. In so doing, Job acknowledges God to be God. This act of submission follows upon what transpires in chaps. 38–41. Only God himself can say who God really is. Only the *encounter* with God himself can purify the praise of God and lead to genuine acknowledgment of God. Ultimately only God himself can say that he is the creator.[1]

The Structure of the Speeches of God

Our starting point is the recognition that the speeches of God in chaps. 38–41 are a development of only *one* motif, namely, praise of the creator, transposed into interrogative form in the mouth of God. Over against this state of affairs the literary question of whether we are dealing here with one divine speech or two (or with three; cf. 40:1–2) is totally secondary. In either case the essential point is the substantive unity of the whole. Likewise, with regard to the question of whether parts of the divine speech(es) might be secondary additions, the important fact remains the determination that the possible additions only further the development of this one motif, going beyond it at not a single point. A further argument for the substantive unity of the divine speech lies in the introduction at 38:1 (= 40:6).[2] The word for "whirlwind" (*ś'rh*) nowhere occurs in the enumeration of the works of creation; it occurs only in the context of either a theophany or a divine judgment.[3] This word probably stems from an ancient theophanic tradition; it also indicates a theophany here. Within the whole of the Job-drama, this theophany *must* have the character of a unique event; there *can only* be one. This must be said irrespective of the "content" of the divine speech. The decisive revelations of God in the Bible always have the character of being unique events. Had a second speech of God out of the whirlwind originally been intended in the plan of the Book of Job, then this second speech would not only have to contain new thoughts (which many interpreters attempt to identify), but it would even have to represent a new act in the drama of the Book of Job—which simply cannot be shown.

With the substantive unity of chaps. 38–41 standing firm, there remain two possibilities for understanding the structure here: either 40:1-14 is no longer in its original location, in which case 40:15 connects directly to 39:30 and the divine speech is unified and without interruption, or 40:15—41:34[26] is open to question in terms of whether or not it originally belonged here. Following the latter course and striking out 40:15—41:34[26], one can interpret 40:7-14 as a conclusion or as originally belonging to the introduction and hence as joining on to 38:2. This attempted solution has only one difficulty: 40:11-13 does not correspond with the introduction. Specifically, these verses contain the only expressions anywhere in chaps. 38–41 that are not in keeping with the motif "praise of the creator." Here in these verses the other aspect of praise of God's majesty is introduced or at least suggested, namely, praise of the lord of history. The precise motif of such praise here voiced is "He topples the mighty from their thrones." Job 40:14 clearly calls to mind Ps. 98:1, right down to the imagery employed; preceding 40:14 is praise of the majesty of God (vv. 9-10). The resulting picture leaves 40:6-14 looking very much like a deliberate and carefully inserted subsequent addition. The whole divine speech is segmented in accord with the psalmic motif: praise of the creator—praise of the lord of history. Therefore the first part must reach its conclusion with 39:30, while the second part begins with 40:6-14. Thus it would be understandable that the introduction in 38:1-3 gets repeated in 40:7-8; the challenge in 38:3 is repeated literally in 40:7, while the reproof in 38:2 is substantially the same as 40:8. This new starting point, necessarily repeating the introductory elements because of the length of chaps. 38–39, would then be a way of emphasizing a deliberate segmentation. However, the development of this second part, "the lord of history," is missing! I can see three possibilities for explaining this lack: (a) The poet wished merely to hint at this second aspect of the hymnic motif, in which case 40:14 is the conclusion of the divine speech and 40:15—41:34[26] is certainly a secondary insertion. (b) The development of the motif has either been broken off and lost, or it was not carried out by the poet, so that there was a gap here from the very beginning. If this was the case it is easy to explain how the description of Behemoth and Leviathan was inserted into this gap. (c) The possibility is not to be excluded that the poet himself deliberately transposed into this setting the description of Behemoth and Leviathan as a veiled development of the motif "God, the lord of history." This would then mean that the two beasts are here meant to embody the great powers of history; they allegorically depict the great powers as seen by the poet of the Book of Job. Thus the poet is saying in a veiled and indirect way that God is the lord also of these historical powers.[4]

Should this third explanation prove acceptable the text could be accepted as transmitted to us (except for 40:1) and intelligently explained in its present order. Above all, the separation of the description of Behemoth and Leviathan from the other descriptions of animals would then be explained as both necessary and meaningful, and 40:7–14 would be fully understandable as an introduction to this description *only.* The repeated introduction in 40:6–7 would then not need to be understood as an introduction to a new speech; it would rather be seen as a way of indicating the caesura between the two parts of the motif at play here. The striking out of 40:6–7 would thus change little in the structure of the whole speech.

If the whole is thus a development of a new motif, namely, praise of the majesty of God the creator (and lord of history), then the structure arises naturally out of this motif:

I. The creator
    1. 38:4–15: God created the world
        4–7: he laid the foundations of the earth
        8–11: he caused the sea to break forth and set bounds for it
        12–15: he let it become light
    2. 38:16–24: God alone knows and oversees the whole creation

16-17: the depths
18-21: the wide places
22-24: the heights
3. 38:24—41:34[26]: God directs and governs his creation
  (a) 38:25-38: in heaven
      25-28: God lets it rain, creates the rain
      29-30: God creates frost, ice, hail
      31-33: God directs the stars
      34-38: God creates the thunder (except v. 36)
  (b) 38:39—41:34[26]: on earth (within which
      is contained Part II: the lord of history)
      39-41:34[26]: God nourishes the animals (lion,
      raven)
      39:1-4: he determines their times (mountain
      goat)
      5-8: he determines for (gives to) them their
      space (wild ass)
      9-12: Addition: intractability (wild ox)
      13-18: speed (ostrich; beginning is missing)
      19-25: ardent strength (horse)
      26-30: ability to fly (hawk, eagle)
II. The lord of history (contained in Part I, 3b)
  (40:6-7: Repetition of the challenging of Job)
    8-10: The Majesty of God, Ruler of the World
    11-13: He brings down the mighty in his wrath
    15-24   ⎫
             ⎬ see below
    25—41:34[26] ⎭

When it is recognized that the structure of the divine speech is a development of this one motif of praise, then it follows that there would have to be a whole series of correlations between this passage and those where praise of the creator is developed elsewhere in the Old Testament. This is in fact the case. All the parallel passages are allied with this same motif. Throughout the Old Testament, divine speech coincides in whole and in part with the motif of praise of the creator. There are only a few clauses from 38:4 to 39:8 which occur only here and nowhere else in the Old Testament; there are only a few clauses in praise of God the creator which occur elsewhere in the Old Testament but are not found in Job 38—39:8. The components of the speech of God were, for the poet of Job, essentially all already at hand in the tradition of this motif. What is peculiar and unique in this speech of God is not really its content but rather its transformation of praise of God (in the language of men) into speech by God. This is just the same as what happened with Deutero-Isaiah (Isa. 44:24; cf. Job 38:4). In both cases this divine speech stands in the context of disputational discourse, in a rejoinder by God; in both cases this rejoinder is directed against an accusation against God, in Deutero-Isaiah it being an accusation of the people and in Job an accusation of an individual.

There are innumerable possibilities for developing the theme of praise of God the creator. And yet, the Old Testament shows that this motif has been restricted, with surprising conformity, to relatively few forms of expression. These forms exhibit a fixed array of expression, an array which admittedly can display considerable variety and whose components for the most part are found only piecemeal, but which never comes down to being merely a capricious enumeration.

The praise of the creator was originally structured by means of verbs, not by nouns; properly speaking, it is not an enumeration of various works of creation but rather an elaboration of the actions of God the creator. The following bifurcation is fundamental:

A. God has created the world (and mankind).
B. God rules over and sustains his creation.

We have gained the impression from Genesis 1 that biblical language with regard to the creation of the world consists essentially of the enumeration of those things which God has created. This impression is misleading; with regard to the question about the Bible's statements on creation, one should not start out from Genesis 1. Over against the "creation narrative" the element of praise of the creator holds primacy of place. In this praise it is the verbs which are decisive, not the direct objects. Part A of the motif of praise of the creator stands isolated in Genesis 1; it can be correctly understood only against the background of the whole motif of praise of the creator.

In Job 38-39 the statements about God's creative activity are restricted to 38:4–11 or 38:4–15; they refer to the earth (vv. 4–7), the sea with its billows (vv. 8–11), and light (vv. 12–15). It is difficult to explain the lack of any reference here to the heavens (such as appears in 9:8). One can vacillate on whether vv. 12–15 belong to A or to B. Yet this much is clear: Part A of this motif functions only as an introduction; what dominates is the divine speech of part B, namely, the part about God's ruling and sustaining his creation. Part B is further bifurcated:

38:25–38: in heaven	as in Psalm 148:	1–6
38:39–41: upon the earth		7–13

An overview has been attached to the beginning of part B; this third part is the prerequisite for the directing and sustaining of such a vast region:

38:16–24: God alone knows (oversees) the whole creation.

This overview is probably a later, reflective expansion upon the praise of the creator; a very similar overview is found in Psalm 139, and it occurs in almost exactly the same format in Sir. 39:19. Here the total created realm is described in terms of its spatial extensions (vv. 16–19: depth; vv. 18–21: breadth; vv. 22–24 height).

With regard to part B, it should be noted that God's rule *in heaven* is extensively described, whereas the description of his rule *on earth* is restricted exclusively to the animal kingdom. This part is obviously governed by a *pars pro toto* pattern of speech. God's actions relating to mankind are completely missing—no doubt intentionally (cf. Ps. 148:7–13).[5] Following 39:8 is an obvious section dealing with God's activity vis-à-vis the animals. Up to this point the poet describes the general necessities for animal life:

38:39–41: God nourishes them (lion, raven)
39:1–4: God determines their times (mountain goat)
39:5–8: God determines their living spaces (wild ass)

So far the types of animals mentioned function only as *examples* for the types of God's activity; instead of lions and ravens, for example, other types of animals could have been named at will. From here on, however, the poet of the Book of Job describes the peculiarities of particular animals or types of animals. Corresponding to this is the fact that the parallels from the rest of the Old Testament coincide with the divine speech up to 39:8. Up to this point the focus of interest is upon God's actions relating to the animals, but from here on the focus imperceptibly shifts to the peculiarities of the animals themselves. The traditional motif of praise is thereby abandoned; now extensions of this motif come to the fore, regardless of whether they originated with our poet himself or were inserted later.[6] Job 39:19–25 and 39:26–30 most closely resemble passages up to 39:8; the queries at the beginning of both these passages (vv. 19 and 26) go back to the element of the praise of God which says, "With him is wisdom and might."

God's work in his creation is described here more extensively than in any other place in the Bible. It is all-encompassing (38:16–24). *Every* activity of God is to be understood on the basis of this overview of the whole in all its dimensions (one might here recall Job's accusation, which reproached God for arbitrary actions). God's activity "on earth as in heaven" obviously has two sides to it: his work in heaven (light, rain, stars, thunder, clouds) has the character of ruling activity; his work on earth quite clearly has the character of providential care. On earth God's wisdom and power bring about life and wholeness and beauty and joy. The God who wonderfully bestows these benefits upon his creatures is the God whose praise is here (indirectly) sung. If now the rule of God on earth is depicted in a *pars pro toto* manner (see above), then one can assume that the poet of Job very subtly intends to suggest in this juxtaposition of heaven and earth also another polarity, one which is otherwise completely lacking in the Book of Job (apart from bits and pieces in the speeches of the friends), namely, that between God's majesty and his goodness. The one-sidedness of the praise of God in Job's speeches consists precisely in the fact that this juxtaposition is missing. Job develops only one side of the polarity which otherwise determines the praise of God in Psalms. Job sees *only* God's majesty (in creation and in history), *not* God's goodness. It is Job's vexation that he can no longer discover the goodness of God in God's work. Now of course it would be in poor taste and hardly possible for the divine speech to contain praise of the goodness of God; our poet's subtlety is shown precisely in the fact that God, *in* the development upon the acts of creation, lets shine through this other side, which finds marvelous expression in the correspondence between his work in heaven and his work on earth. Likewise, this aspect can be seen only if one compares the parallels within the common motif; that God "gives food to all flesh" goes along with the general praise of his goodness.[7] Thus these words, as a message directed to Job, contain in addition to their reproof a very quiet, reserved, and yet obvious allusion to God's providential goodness, by which he works for the sake of his creatures—and not just for the animals.

Behemoth and Leviathan

How do the poems about Behemoth and Leviathan relate to the material that precedes them; in what way are they connected to it? Initially, let us hold on to the possibility that the text is to be taken in its present shape, assuming that 40:15—41:34[26] can be read as following upon 40:6-14. In 38:2 the reproof reads "Who is this that darkens counsel . . . ?" God's "decree," his plan, is then unfolded in the works of his creation.[8] In 40:8 the reproof reads "Will you shatter my judgment, will you put me in the wrong, that you may be justified?" This is legal terminology, and it can refer only to God's actions toward *human beings* in the historical sphere. Job 40:11-13 confirms this; God in his anger brings down the imperious. Verse 11b is quite similar to Isa. 2:11-17; the Hebrew word $g\bar{e}'eh$ ("one that is proud") appears in the same form in Isa. 2:12. (Cf. also Ps. 94:2: "Rise up, O judge of the earth; render to the proud their deserts!") In v. 12 these proud ones are also described as "the wicked." However, the reference here is certainly to the decisive acts of God in the realm of human history: God topples those who have elevated themselves too high (in relation to other people and against God). One now expects this activity of God to be developed in a fashion similar to what happens at 38:2 in the section comprised by chaps. 38-39. But this does not happen. Instead there is a description of two beasts, *apparently* as a continuation of the series of animals mentioned in chaps. 38-39. Can these descriptions of the two beasts be understood as a *veiled* reference to God's actions in history? The fact that the hippopotamus and the crocodile are obviously described as "mighty" creatures, to a degree which sets them apart from all the previously mentioned animals, could speak in favor of this interpretation. Arguing against this possibility, however, is the fact that there is absolutely no talk about God's sovereignty over these mighty ones, specifically that he topples them or forces them back within their own domains. On the contrary, the talk about these beasts is apparently with regard only to their being the most powerful of God's *creatures.* Thus the descriptions of these two beasts belong with the series of animal descriptions of chap. 39.

With regard to Behemoth (40:15-24), not only the text but also the arrangement of the verses is badly disrupted.[9] There is lacking *any* element by which this description is worked into an address directed to Job (cf. 39:13-18). There is no specific designation of this as a speech of God, nor is there any reference here to a particular act of God with regard to this beast. The sole point of reference to the broader context here lies in the characterizing of this beast as a particularly strong, powerful animal. To me, the decisive consideration seems to be that after the introduction in 40:6-14 one expects to find here some reference to a distinct act of God (e.g., he topples the mighty). However, the description in 40:15-24 reveals not the slightest indication of such a reference; the description says only that this powerful creature belongs to God's created order (perhaps also that God created Behemoth to lord it over the other creatures—but this is only conjecture).

The passage about Leviathan (41:1-34 [40:25—41:26]) differs from 40:15-24 first of all in that it is cast *totally* as an address directed to Job, from 41:1 [40:25] all the way to 41:8 [40:32]. From there on the address to Job ceases and the passage becomes mere description as in 40:15-24. The basic problem for this whole passage lies in 41:10-11 [41:2-3]. Here one suddenly encounters first-person speech, which is to say divine speech, without introduction and apparently without any connection to what goes before or comes after. If the use of the first person here is a textual error, as most modern exegetes maintain, then through removal of this disruption the whole—namely, 41:1-34 [40:25—41:26]—is restored as a large, uninterrupted, unified, and thorough description of Leviathan. On the other hand, if one cannot agree with the reasons for changing this first-person speech into third-person language in

41:10–11 [41:2–3], then this section becomes decisive for the under-standing of the whole speech of God.

The Conclusion of the Speech of God

Let us first of all take a look at the overall structure:[10]

41:1–8 (& v. 9?): Address to Job
  1–2: Can you capture him? (also v. 7)
  3–4: Can you persuade him to become your servant?
    5: Can you make him into a plaything?
    6: Can you use him as an item of exchange?
  8 (& 9?): Answer: Try it. Surely you will not succeed!
    6: Can you use him as an item of exchange?

41:10–11: *either:* No one can stand against him
          or: (10a) Conclusion of the preceding: No one . . .
          (10b–11) Deduction: Who can stand up to me
          (God)?

41:12–34: Description of the beast
   12: *either* the conclusion of vv. 10–11 *or* a new starting point
  13–14: Who penetrates his armor? Who opens his jaws?
  15–17: The armor on his back
  18–21: He spews fire out of all his orifices
  23–24: His flesh, his heart
  22&25: He spreads abroad fear and terror
  26–29: He is unassailable
  30–32: His way upon land and in water
  33–34: He is unique in his fearsomeness

1. Description of his body: 12–17, 23–24
2. Description of his movement, his activity:
  a. He spews out fire: 18–21
  b. His movement: 30–32
3. He spreads abroad fear and terror: 22&25; the effect
4. He is unassailable: 26–29
5. Conclusion: the unique, the dominant one: 33–34

If one starts out by inquiring after the context of the two parts or after their relationship to each other, one arrives at the certain conclusion that the two do not form a unity. In no case do we have here a homogeneous series of statements about Leviathan. That is clearly shown when one compares 41:1-2, 7 with 41:26-29. Both passages deal with overpowering the beast, either to take it captive or to slay it. The means employed are quite different in the two places; 41:1-2, 7 clearly presupposes that we are dealing with an aquatic beast. However, if one were to read 41:26-29 on its own terms, no one would conclude that the beast in question is an aquatic one; the weapons mentioned are of the sort one uses *only* on land. Given the vivid and detailed descriptions of these two fundamentally different methods of gaining control over the beast, one cannot simply take their juxtaposition for granted. However, another difference is even more crucial. There is *absolutely* no description of the beast in the address to Job in 41:1-8—not a single word. Instead, the concern here is exclusively with the *encounter* of the addressee with Leviathan. Moreover, the description of the beast really begins only in 41:12 (or 13) and goes on uninterruptedly from there to the conclusion, thereby corresponding fully to the pattern in 40:15-23. In other words, 41:1-8 obviously stands out from the overall section comprised of 40:15—41:32. This passage alone is an address to an opponent; only this section deals with the relationship of the addressee to Leviathan.

Now one must inquire about 41:10-11. If it is true that 41:1-8 (& v. 9?) stands out from the whole as a separate passage, then the question about the proper reading of these two verses arises in a new form. That divine speech in the first person suddenly crops up here would then be unintelligible and hardly acceptable as the original text only under the condition that the real matter at hand was a continuous description of Leviathan, into the midst of which these extraneous verses abruptly intruded. From such a perspective it is thoroughly understandable how most recent interpretations alter the first-person speech into a third-person form. However, when 41:1-9 is read strictly on its own terms, then 41:10-11 becomes the conclusion to this section. And not only that, but—if 40:15-24 and 41:12-32 are later insertions—41:10-11 then also becomes *the conclusion to the whole speech of God!* As such these verses are not only in every way intelligible but also then the solution to a difficulty which has long been recognized, namely, that it is hard to understand how the speech of God could originally have ended with 41:32. Given the minutely planned and painstakingly executed structure of the Book of Job, it can hardly be assumed that the speech of God, which began with such intensity as an *address* to Job, should subside into such a mere description at the end and conclude without any indication of being the culmination of an address. It is not just the length of the description of Leviathan as such which raises questions, but even more its total lack of any characteristics of an address.

There are several reasons why it is probable that 41:10–11 is the original conclusion to the speech of God. (a) The first reason is textual. Driver and Gray correctly note that the first-person suffixes in vv. 10b and 11a are hardly understandable as subsequent alterations of originally third-person suffixes, and that the identical textual disruption is not likely to have occurred twice in a row.[11] (b) Especially if we join the many who read *mî hû'* ["who is he"] in place of the text's *lî hû'* ["it is mine"]—but even apart from this change—the conclusion of the speech of God then clearly points back to its beginning: "Who is this that darkens counsel . . . ?" Such a circling back to the beginning at the conclusion of a section of speech is characteristic of the Book of Job. Thus the conclusion of the second section of divine speech, 41:10–11, would correspond to the conclusion of the first section at 40:1. (c) This conclusion to the speech of God clearly refers back to an utterance of Job occurring precisely at the place where Job takes up for the first time the very same motif of "praise of the majesty of God":

> Wise of mind and mighty in strength;
> who could rebel against him and remain unscathed? (9:4)

The resounding of this expression *there* in the mouth of Job and *here* in what is said by God to Job would be just one more fine detail in the tying together of the parts. (d) The most important argument is that now, at the end of his speech, God indirectly answers the charge Job has undertaken against him:

> . . . Let the Almighty answer me!
> . . . Like a prince I would approach him! (31:35–37)

Directly following these words of Job is God's "Who is this that
. . ." (38:2); the whole ends with this same rebuke: ". . . under the
whole heaven, who might he be?" [41:11b]. But just before this
expression stands the clause "Who has stood up to me and remained unscathed?" [41:11a]. Herein lies intimated the *real*—albeit
unspoken—conclusion to the speech of God: Job has remained unscathed; God has not shattered him to bits.

So how is the whole second part of the speech of God to be
understood, namely, the part introduced by 40:6–14, developed by
the short passage in 41:1–9, and concluded by 41:10–11? Job
40:6–14 introduces the praise of "God, the lord of history," which
is the second element in the praise of the majesty of God. Only *one*
motif from this element is mentioned: he topples the mighty (missing is the motif of elevating the lowly). This motif does not get
explicitly developed in what follows; apparently what gets continued is indirect praise of the creator. However, in keeping with the
new introduction, the topic now shifts to the mighty among the
animals. Hence direct address to Job, as immediate continuation of
what precedes, is found only in 41:1–11. The questions here directed to Job are different from the questions in the first part of the
speech of God. There they all come out meaning, in effect, "Did
you participate in the creation? Are you capable of taking part in
the preservation and governance of the creation?" These questions
therefore correspond to the first part of the praise motif. The questions in the second part, on the other hand (see above, p. 111), are
all directed toward a historical event taken in the broadest sense of
the term. Here they all come down to the question "Can you become the master of these mighty ones?" Bluntly stated: "Job, in
God's creation there are beings so powerful that you, despite your
best efforts, must necessarily fail to become their master." There is
also here an indirect reference to the mighty and the powerful, the
ones of whom the introduction said that God is able to topple them
from their thrones. One expects at the conclusion a question such
as "Are you perhaps able to . . . ?" which the divine speech would
then develop along the lines of either "Also these mighty ones have
I created" (cf. 40:15) or "I can annihilate them in a moment."
What happens, however, is that the direct relationship of God to
these mighty ones gets passed over; instead, a conclusion is drawn

following the principle of *a minore ad maius:* since no one can stand up against these mighty creatures, who could possibly stand up against God (41:10)? In my opinion this abrupt and disjointed transition is intelligible only if one still hears, behind the development in 41:1–11, the clauses of that motif which is here being developed and which still determines the whole, namely, the motif "God overthrows the mighty." Thus 41:10b is to be heard in this way: Who could ever stand up against God, to whom belongs the office of overthrowing the mighty? Put another way, the question directed to Job throughout 41:1–14 ("Are you perhaps able to . . . ?") demands the unspoken answer "No [41:8], you cannot possibly succeed here—only God can [41:11–13]!"

There remains the question of why the activity of God in the historical realm is pointed out with reference to a creature and not a real historical power. I am not able to answer this question with certainty. However, it is possible that, in the speech directed to Job, the question of whether Job was in a position to stand up against some historical superpower would have had a clumsy effect. On the other side of the coin, it is *precisely* in its current format that the speech of God arrives at such a remarkable inclusiveness. Moreover, as a comparison with Ps. 104:26 shows, our poet here plays along with a preexistent tradition which is accustomed to mention Leviathan at the conclusion of a series of enumerations. Why this should happen is also something which cannot be answered with certainty, but what remains decisive is the fact that the questions put to Job in 41:1–7 differ from those put to him in 38:4ff. This difference in questions helps clearly to separate the second part of the divine speech, introduced by 40:6–14, from the first part of this speech. The new introduction is thereby understandable, and it seems to me certain that, behind this dichotomy in the speech of God, there stands the dichotomy within the underlying motif drawn from the praise of God (praise of the creator—praise of the lord of history). The resulting explanation shows that the new introduction is to be taken as only an indicator of this dichotomy and not as something which destroys the overall unity of God's answer to Job. The conclusion to this answer of God is thus to be seen in 41:10–11. This is a genuine conclusion to the divine speech, obviously referring back to the beginning of the speech and even going back to Job's summoning of God prior to the start of the divine speech. It is upon *these* words in 41:10–11 that Job's answer directly follows.

Thus, in the speech of God the following are to be regarded as later, secondary additions: 39:9–12, probably also 39:13–30, 40:15–24, and 41:12–34. Whether these passages were appended by the poet of the Book of Job himself or by a later hand can hardly be determined. These passages betray the tendency, visible at several places, of passing over from praise of the creator to description of what has been created (cf. n. 6).

NOTES

1. The transition from praise of God to divine speech has an obvious correspondence in Deutero-Isaiah; cf., e.g., Isa. 44:24.

2. Job 40:1–2 can in no way present a separate speech of God. If one judges that the text here is intact, then it can only be a concluding resumption of 38:1. Job 38:1 and 40:2 would then be like a set of parentheses that is supposed to bracket the lengthy speech of God. Job 40:1, which is lacking in the Septuagint, should be stricken.

3. Cf. esp. 2 Kings 2:1, 11; Ezek. 1:4; 13:13.

4. Our interpretation here can appeal for support to a tradition attested in the Old Testament. In Isa. 27:1 Behemoth and Leviathan represent the dominant world powers of that time. To be sure, this passage is probably later than Job. However, the world powers are spoken of in mythic terminology in such a way that it is certainly to be assumed that an already preexistent tradition has here been taken up—a tradition which therefore can also have been available to the poet of Job. The customary alternative when it comes to interpreting these two beasts, namely, that they are either real beasts or they are mythic beings (most modern interpreters decide in favor of the first alternative; cf., e.g., Karl Budde [*Das Buch Hiob*, Handkommentar zum Alten Testament 2/1 (Göttingen, ²1913)] against Hermann Gunkel ["Hiobbuch," in *Die Religion in Geschichte und Gegenwart* (Tübingen, ²1929)]), thus misses the real intent of this section of the divine speech. Admittedly we are here dealing with a description of real, flesh-and-blood animals, at the mention of whose names the hearers recall the mythic monsters who were vanquished in primordial battle (Gunkel). However, this allusion to the mythic creatures of the primordial battle against chaos has here the intent of directing attention, by means of these two creatures of God's creation, to the powers of contemporary history whom no one can restrain and yet whose lord is the One who created them; these beasts are portrayed *in the place of* the historical powers. In an indi-

rect and concealed way, praise is also thereby rendered to the lord of history. Put another way, the allusion to the creatures of chaos, the mythic enemies of the Creator-God, does not intend merely to refer to these creatures as such. The real focus of interest is upon the battle waged by the Creator-God. It is not only the passage in Isa. 27:1 which shows that reference to Behemoth and Leviathan can also refer to God's victory over the great powers of history; there is also such a passage in Deutero-Isaiah, one which is certainly older than the Job-poem. In the stylized lament song in Isa. 51:9-11, the people remind their God: "Was it not thou that didst cut Rahab in pieces, that didst pierce the dragon?" They do this in hopes of prompting God's present intervention in history in order to protect his people from the great powers. The answer to this lament song is a salvation oracle promising just such intervention of God (vv. 17, 23). It is possible that the starting point lies here for the practice of designating the world powers by means of the chaos monsters.

5. On the other hand, one cannot say that there is no mention of vegetation; God's activity relating to the plant world is circumscribed by his providing nourishment for the plants, which is mentioned in vv. 26-27 and 37-38.

6. In the matter of these expansions, we could well be dealing with the appearance of a whole new motif, namely, that of "naturalistic wisdom." Albrecht Alt was the first to set out the importance of this motif for the Old Testament ("Die Weisheit Salomos," *Theologische Literaturzeitung* 76 [1951]: 139-44); in addition to the numerical proverbs in Proverbs 30, he assigns the divine speeches in the Book of Job to this category. But such a succinct statement simply does not hold true; the origin of Job 38—39:8 in praise of God can certainly be demonstrated. However, Alt's determination of this material as naturalistic wisdom can apply correctly to the expansions. A similar case is to be found in Sirach 39, where praise of God is expanded in the direction of this naturalistic wisdom.

7. Cf. Ps. 136:23-25; 145:13b-15; 104:24, 27; 147:9-11.

8. It is perhaps not accidental that at the end of this section there stands a work relating to the insight of God (39:26) [*sic*].

9. Behemoth's manner of living is described in vv. 15b, 20(?), 21-23; his strength is depicted in vv. 16-18, in connection with the description of his bodily components; his significance is mentioned in v. 19; v. 24 remains open to question (a reference to the impossibility of capturing him?).

10. [In this section we will follow the versification as it appears in English translations, without including the Hebrew versification in brackets.—Trans.]

11. Samuel R. Driver and George Buchanan Gray, *The Book of Job,* International Critical Commentary 10, 11 (Edinburgh, 1921).

10

Job's Answer

The question has so far been left open as to whether Job answered God once or twice (40:3–5 and 42:1–6). However, the answer to this question results from what has been said about the speech of God. Just as the speech of God, in keeping with its nature as theophany, can only be *one,* so also Job's final utterance in answer to this speech of God can only be one. The same conclusion results necessarily from the structure of the whole. However, it is not therefore necessary to alter the text, according to which both speak twice. The bifurcation in the divine speech results from the dichotomy in the underlying motif. That Job apparently answers twice is simply an adjustment to this twofold state of affairs; substantively speaking, there is here only *one* answer. The only question which might be raised is whether the two parts of the answer are particularly related to the corresponding two parts of the divine speech. The first part of the answer (40:3–5) is of one piece; everything Job here says is really expressed as soon as he makes the gesture in v. 4b: Job must be silent. With this gesture it is already clear that Job's answer is in fact only *one* answer, even though one may go on to leave the text precisely as it has been transmitted to us. Job 40:4–5 is not, strictly speaking, an answer; it is an act of silencing which precedes the answer itself. It is against the background of this act of silencing that the answer itself in 42:2–6 stands. This gesture is also a sign which serves only to confirm the dichotomy found here as being a bifurcation of *one* speech and *one* answer.

It is generally recognized that the text of 42:2–6 is disrupted. I follow the conjecture of Stier,[1] who reads *higgaḏtānî* ["you have made known to me"] in place of the text's *higgaḏtî* ["I have uttered"] in v. 3 and who inserts the *gəḏōlôṯ* ["great things"] preserved in the Septuagint:

> I know that you can do all things,
>   and that no purpose of yours can be thwarted. (v. 2)
> "You" have made known "great things" "to me" which I did not
>   comprehend;
>   things too wonderful for me, which I did not understand. (v. 3b)
> I had heard of you by the hearing of the ear,
>   but now my eye has seen you. (v. 5)
> Therefore "I dissolve in tears,"
>   and repent in dust and ashes. (v. 6)

Not too much can be built upon the interpretation of v. 6; it is textually uncertain, and the usual interpretation to the effect that Job here adopts the behavior of a penitent is quite uncertain. Here also, Stier's way of reading the verse is noteworthy. While the part of the answer appearing in 40:4–5 was dominated by "I" as the subject, in 42:2–6 the controlling point of reference is God. It is very difficult to arrive at an exact understanding of this answer in 42:2–6. The key to its interpretation lies once again in the motif which underlies these words. This is clearly recognizable. Verses 2 and 3b contain words that praise God. Verse 2 is praise of God's omnipotence; very often one finds in Psalms praise of the God who does great and wonderful things.[2] This motif shows up frequently (especially in the beginnings of psalms), and the parallelism "great—wonderful" so obviously points to this specific theme from the praise of God that the same theme is certainly intended to resonate in this portion of Job's answer. Now it is the case, however, that the expression *niplā'ôṯ* ["wonderful things"/"wonders"] appears in Psalms in a very definite context. This is best shown by Gideon's question to the messenger of God in Judg. 6:13: "And where are all his wonderful deeds, which our fathers . . . ?" The descriptive psalm of praise tells of these wonders: "I will tell of all thy wonderful deeds . . ." (Ps. 9:1[2]). Here and in many other places what is meant by *niplā'ôṯ* is God's wonderful deeds for the benefit of his people or for his righteous adherents. On one occasion the concept parallel to *niplā'ôṯ* is *ḥăsāḏêḵā* ["thy steadfast love"]: "Our fathers . . . did not consider thy wonderful works, and they did not remember the abundance of thy steadfast love"

(Ps. 106:7). The upshot of all this is that the great and wonderful thing which God made known to Job and which Job did not comprehend is not just any old thing, nor is it only God's work as creator. On the contrary, it is precisely that which Gideon meant by this word, namely, God's wonderful intervention on behalf of his people, the deeds of God upon which Israel's history rests (Ps. 106:7).[3] All this is difficult to perceive here in the case of Job, since what God makes known to Job are actually works of the creator. And yet the use of *niplā'ôt* here corresponds perfectly with the understanding of the speech of God which we have worked out; according to our interpretation, the second part of God's speech deals with God's governance in history. To be sure, it shows only the one aspect, namely, that God is lord over the powerful; the other aspect of God's activity is only intimated in 38:39—39:8, namely, that he sustains and preserves his creatures. That the side comprising God's saving activity, his compassion, his providence, and his forgiveness must be left out of the divine speech is based in the structure of the whole composition. This is the side which Job, reeling from his blows, simply cannot hear or understand in his situation. In the Job-drama God's saving activity is concentrated on one single point: God did answer Job. Therein alone did Job experience God's goodness, and therein he experienced it fully. However, this is *not* stated explicitly; it is only hinted at. Job was not able to understand that the God who had created him and then thrust him into the depths, who created this world as it is, could be the gracious, helping, saving God; this was "too wonderful" for him (42:3b). Now he has comprehended it; now he knows it. *Yd'* ["to know"] has in any case one meaning which is recognizable without further ado. By this word it cannot—or at least can not only—be meant that God has made something understandable to Job by means of the divine speech, for nothing was said in this speech of which Job did not already know the content. All the statements here have their parallels in the praise of the creator. This "to know" is rather to be understood as parallel to v. 5b: "But now my eye has seen you." God's self-revelation, the encounter with God, the very fact that God has answered Job and *not* destroyed him—this has given Job the understanding he had lost. What is therefore meant here is "to know" in its full sense, in the sense which encompasses one's total existence. Perhaps one can hear even more of the meaning of *yəḏa'tî* ["I knew"] from a parallel in Psalms. We found that God's answer to Job corresponds to places in Psalms at which at one time the salvation oracle stood (see above). In several places the supplicant's answer to this salvation oracle begins, "Now I know that. . . ."

> Now I know that the Lord will help his anointed;
>   he will answer him. . . . (Ps. 20:6[7])

> This I know, that God is for me. (Ps. 56:9[10])

> I know that the Lord maintains the cause of the afflicted. . . .
>   (Ps. 140:12[13])

> By this I know that thou art pleased with me. . . . (Ps. 41:11[12])

Psalm 135:5–6 offers a near parallel to Job 42:2–3:

> For I know that the Lord is great. . . .
> Whatever the Lord pleases he does, in heaven and on earth.

Whether the statement directed to God, "I know that you . . . ," has been diverted to here from the answer to the salvation oracle in the descriptive psalm of praise would be difficult to prove. Our concern here is only with the fact of the substantive parallel. Job's "I know that . . ." in his answer, along with his statement in v. 5b, is to be understood as something which has grown out of his encounter with God and not as a mere act of intellectual recognition. Likewise the words "But now my eye has seen you" ought not to be flattened out; what is meant is not so much a "meaningful experience" in our modern sense as an encounter in the personal sense, just as the Bible can elsewhere speak, for example, of "seeing" salvation. This verse at 42:5 contains the "solution" to the "problem" of Job. There is no other. God has answered Job. God has met Job. Insofar as Job attests to this, he attests to the reality of God in its wholeness. Now he knows God, and no longer just one aspect of God's activity. That Job refrains from saying this, that *what* Job has recognized and *whom* he has seen remains concealed, is one mark of the real greatness of this work. Verse 6 suggests the effect on Job of his encounter with God. It corresponds to 40:4–5. There Job is silenced; here he is unnerved ("I melt into tears") by the encounter and bows before God.

This confession of Job is the conclusion of the drama. The epilogue which still follows necessarily belongs, as does the prologue, to the whole. The midpoint of the epilogue is the clause in v. 10a: "And the Lord restored the fortunes of Job." This clause is a necessary part of God's answering of Job. God *has* answered Job, and thereby the change in his fate has already been determined and has already begun to be realized. However, since the whole is a report of an event, it must now also be affirmed that these other things followed, just as happens in narrative praise (see above, p. 107). Everything that follows in vv. 10b-17 is merely development of v. 10a. Preceding this is an utterance of God directed to the friends about what must yet take place. For the role of the friends, representing one person in the drama, was abruptly broken off with Eliphaz's accusation of Job in chap. 22. That higher court before which Job then had to take his case must now take a stance regarding this judgment of the friends. An especially impressive feature of the forgiving goodness of God comes to the fore right at this point: the friends experience the collapse of their theology precisely in that *they* are forgiven. They should indeed not be disconcerted that Job is selected as the mediator of this forgiveness to them. God made known to Job something which he had never before understood, and God does exactly the same for the friends. In that God "lifted up the head" of Job, the *friends* were also helped. Like Job they stand over against the living God, before whom pious dogma is shattered just as much as is indignant lamentation, and before whom the friends can only join Job in bowing down and saying to him, "Yes."

NOTES

1. Fridolin Stier, *Das Buch Ijjob, hebräisch und deutsch* (Munich: Kosel, 1954), pp. 351-52.
2. Cf. Ps. 106:21-22; 136:4; 98:1; 111:2-4; 1 Chron. 16:24.
3. As far as I can tell, God's activity as creator is never conceived of with the word *niplā'ôt*.

11

Chapters 24–27: Fragments

When one attempts to survey the discussion of these chapters 24–27 according to the compilations by Pfeiffer, Eissfeldt, Budde, and now Kuhl, one would most like to renounce entirely any new attempt at a solution. It seems to me that particularly the outstandingly comprehensive description by Kuhl points out one thing for sure: as they have been transmitted to us, these chapters simply *cannot* present us with a unified text. If unanimity can be achieved in this matter, then we have taken an important step, for then it would be acknowledged that fragments appear in these chapters— and at least initially the question can remain quite open of just how much material in these chapters is fragmentary and what the character of these fragments is. The next step would then be to ask whether there is some fixed point from which a determination and a delimitation of these fragments would be possible. However, since at the outset everything in chaps. 24–27 is uncertain, this fixed point would have to lie *outside* these chapters themselves. In my opinion such a fixed point is to be found in the fact that the third cycle of discourse consists of only *one* speech by a friend (chap. 22) and *one* speech by Job (chap. 23). Ignoring at the time chaps. 24–27, our earlier investigation came to this conclusion on the basis of the structure of the disputational discourse as a whole and the speeches of both Job and Eliphaz which conclude the disputational discourse (see above, p. 27). On the basis of this investigation, and not primarily from the questionability of chaps. 24–27, we concluded that a continuation beyond chaps. 22 and 23 of the disputational discourse is not to be assumed. The third step toward gaining this fixed point, after the delimiting of the individual fragments, is then to inquire after their character and their original setting. More reliable viewpoints for this third line of questioning have been won from what has gone before through the precise determination of the forms of speech throughout the Book of Job. Looking back upon the preceding discussion, one can certainly say that a reconstruction of the third cycle of discourse *after* chap. 23, or in other words a second and a third speech by a friend and by Job, has hardly been successfully achieved. The proffered results differ so greatly and are so conjectural that, to date, not one of these attempted reconstructions has proved convincing. However, if the attempt at such precise reconstruction is abandoned the whole inquiry is considerably simplified. If a fragment is recognizable in terms of its boundaries and its form of speech, the first question to be asked is whether it could belong to one of the earlier speeches in the disputational discourse or whether it must be regarded as an increment alien to this discourse. Of course, the degree of certainty with which the original context can be determined varies; it seems to me that a precise determination can be made with regard to chaps. 25–26, 27:2–6, and 27:13–23. Kuhl's question is legitimate, namely, "How is one supposed to take transpositions of such great magnitude and make them intelligible?"[1] We are dealing in chaps. 24–27 with *unfinished* fragments; the most one can say is that they were meant for this or that place.

When we dealt with the final speech of Job we demonstrated how this speech probably ends with 23:17. It is generally recognized that chap. 24 offers within itself no recognizable context. That this chapter belongs to the final speech of Job within the dialogue section is highly unlikely. Chapter 24 consists of a series of fragments:

1. Verses 1–4, 9 (12?), 22, 23, 25: Why is God found on the side of the transgressor, not hindering his activity? This is a fragment belonging to chap. 21, or in any case corresponding to that chapter (see above, p. 95, n. 19).

2. Verses 5–11 (except v. 9): A description of a group of refugees; this is an expansion which has no original setting either in the speeches of Job or in those of the friends.

3. Verses 13–17: A comprehensive, observant description of the "enemy of light" in the manner of the Proverbs; alien to the Book of Job.

4. Verses 18–20, 24: The end of a transgressor; given the similarity to the same motif in the speeches of the friends, this could well be a fragment from one of those speeches.

The resulting picture here is certainly one of an accumulation of broken pieces. However, if chap. 23 is the concluding speech of Job and the conclusion to the dialogue section as a whole—as we learned above—then the presence of these fragments can in no way alter the fact that by this point the dialogue section is essentially completed.

When we dealt with the motif of the "praise of God" in the speeches of the friends (see above, p. 77), we found that the original place for chaps. 25–26 was the first speech of Bildad, chap. 8. Job 26:1–4 also belongs there as the probable beginning of the speech of Job which now follows in chap. 9. Both the text and the superscriptions have been preserved; all that is necessary is a simple transposition: 26:1–4 is to be read after 26:5–14 (see above, p. 78).

Our analysis of chap. 27 yields these results:

1. Verses 2–6 are probably the beginning of the oath of clearance in chap. 31 (see above, p. 98).

2. Verses 13–23 depict the fate of the transgressor, fully in the style of the speeches of the friends; the same motif is found in vv. 8–10, namely, that the transgressor is without hope. This material probably belongs in the first speech of Zophar in chap. 11, though it is difficult to determine whether vv. 8–10 are really a part of this material (see above, p. 93, n. 1).

3. Two small pieces remain very questionable. Does v. 7 belong to Job's oath of clearance? That is a possibility, although 31:1 ties in better with 27:6. Another context for this particular verse is not to be found. Verses 11-12 introduce a speech and, to be sure, a speech where one person addresses several others. However, these two verses do not sound like the beginning of a speech of Job. On the other hand, they do fairly obviously sound like something from the Elihu speeches, more specifically the long introductory speech in chap. 32. It is possible that these two verses are the introduction to chap. 28.[2]

In conclusion, chaps. 25–26 in their entirety—and most of chap. 27—contain portions of speeches by Job and the friends. Only chap. 24 is a collection of numerous individual pieces, of which two probably belonged to the original composition of the Book of Job while two definitely did not.[3]

NOTES

1. Curt Kuhl, "Neuere Literarkritik des Buches Hiob," *Theologische Rundschau,* N.F. 21 (1953): 279.

2. Thus Johannes Lindblom (*La composition du livre de Job* [Lund: C. W. K. Gleerup, 1945]), Eduard König (*Das Buch Hiob* [Gütersloh, 1929]), A. Lefèvre ("Le livre de Job," in Supplément au Dictionnaire de la Bible, ed. André Robert, vol. 4, cols. 1073–98 [Paris: Librairie Letouzey et Ané, 1949]), and Kuhl ("Literarkritik," p. 281). This would explain the *kî* in 28:1, but who is supposed to be the speaker?

3. The exegesis of these chapters 24–27 shows how an interpretation which holds fast to the transmitted text at all costs and wishes to deny the presence of disruptions, flaws, and disorder is forced into hypotheses which are often wide of the mark and harmonizations based in the exegete's own imagination; cf. my review of Möller (Hans W. Möller, *Sinn und Aufbau des Buches Hiob* [Berlin: Evangelische Verlagsanstalt, 1955]) in *Zeichen der Zeit* (1955): 10.

12

Chapter 28

At least initially this poem is to be heard and understood on its own terms.[1] The poem is an expansion on a short proverb which consists of a question (v. 12 = v. 20) and an answer (v. 23); in other words, it is a riddle, consisting of a problem and its solution. Everything else here is readily understandable as expansion upon the question and the answer. The answer has a positive aspect (v. 23) and a negative aspect (v. 13 = v. 21). There is an explanatory development of the positive side in vv. 24–27. The negative side is further expanded in the direction of two possibilities for achieving wisdom: one might try to attain wisdom either through investigation or through purchase. The possibility of the latter is directly denied; even the greatest valuables cannot be exchanged for wisdom (vv. 15–19).[2] The possibility of the former is denied through the use of an image. Mankind has successfully compelled the earth to open access to her subterranean treasures (vv. 1–11), but no human skill, discovery, or technique can force access to wisdom. In other words, the discussion here focuses upon those two means by which human beings, then as now, can best unlock problems and open up new possibilities: wealth and technology. However, both these forces only represent a development of the *negative* answer; neither gives mankind *any* access to wisdom. The access to wisdom lies beyond even the greatest potentialities of mankind; "It is hid from the eyes of all living." But all this is only the negative background to the real affirmation of the proverb or poem. The real answer to the question here raised is that *God* knows the place of wisdom and exercises control over the access to it, for he is the creator (vv. 24–27).

In terms of its form, chap. 28 stands apart from its surroundings. It belongs to none of the forms of speech that underlie the Book of Job. Chapter 28 can be neither a speech by one of the

135

friends nor a speech by Job, nor indeed is it introduced as such. Neither can it represent the high point of the book, as some interpreters assume;[3] this is rendered impossible already by its location *before* the great concluding lament. This chapter—and this chapter alone in the whole Book of Job—is comprised of pure wisdom speech. As was shown above, this chapter is to be understood as an expansion of *one* proverb:

> Where shall wisdom be found?
>   And where is the place of understanding?
> It is hid from the eyes of all living,
>   and concealed from the birds of the air. . . .
> God understands the way to it, and he knows its place.

The same structure is shown, for example, in Proverbs and Ecclesiastes:

> Who has woe? Who has sorrow?
>   Who has strife? Who has complaining? . . .
> Those who tarry long over wine,
>   those who go to try mixed drink. (Prov. 23:29-30)

> Who is like the wise man?
> And who knows the interpretation of a thing?
> A man's wisdom makes his face shine,
>   and the hardness of his countenance is changed.[4] (Eccles. 8:1)

However, more important than these parallels to the individual proverb disclosed by Job 28 is the elaboration upon individual proverbs to make up whole poems as displayed at many places in the Book of Proverbs. Most of the wisdom poems in Proverbs 1-9 are expanded admonitions or warnings. One can observe precisely how the course of development leads from individual proverbs cast in basic parallel form to poems of two lines, three lines, and so on all the way to poems of more than ten lines. The process of expansion is for the most part extremely simple and easily understood. Less common are the expansions on proverbs cast in the form of statements, although there are some to be found (e.g., Prov. 31:10ff.). The question needs to be raised whether the descriptive poem (the lyric poem) has not perhaps grown out of the descriptive proverb cast in statement form.

Now that Job 28 has been explained in terms of its form we must turn to the question of its function in its current setting. Substantively speaking, Job 28 admittedly does not correspond at all to the customary wisdom speech, and it stands in sharp contrast to the praise of wisdom as found, for example, in Proverbs 1–9. Occasionally in Proverbs there is a hint of skepticism regarding wisdom, as in 21:30. This skepticism is more pronounced in Ecclesiastes; however, even there it never finds such radical expression as in Job 28. Job 28 dares to maintain that mankind is never able to gain disposal of wisdom, because mankind does not know how to arrive at wisdom and possesses no medium of exchange by which to purchase it. All this stands in opposition to the frequent admonition to "acquire wisdom" in Proverbs 1–9 (e.g., 4:5); it is nothing less than a revolutionary thesis: wisdom cannot be acquired! This thesis is obviously directed against a kind of certainty that thinks it can gain absolute control over the standards of thought and action. The message thrown in the face of this certainty is that such control over wisdom is possible only for the creator, never for the creature. Wisdom never becomes a human possession.

This radical, polemical thesis makes good sense where it stands in the Book of Job. It is an intermezzo in the pause between the first and second acts of the drama, a concluding response to the speeches of the friends. To be sure, the final word can be spoken only at the end by the higher court (42:7–9). However, there is certainly a place for a concluding response to the speeches of the friends, one which follows directly upon their final utterance and which in a certain sense accompanies their departure from the stage. The friends thought they had fixed standards at their disposal and could use them to make a judgment upon Job, and this is what they did. However, the final judgment on the matter was that they did not speak rightly of God. Why? Chapter 28 gives the answer: Wisdom is not at human disposal in the sure way the friends assumed and presupposed it was. In the speeches of the friends, the poet of the Book of Job allows a distinct theology of his time to find expression. Chapter 28 is a final word on this sort of theology; it is the radical combating of a theology which thinks it has information, in the form of available wisdom, about God's dealings with mankind.[5]

Thus there is no reason to deny that this chap. 28 was part of the original plan of the Book of Job. It is precisely in its foreignness, in its departure from the style of the disputation speeches, that this chapter has its significance; in its place it plays the role of a *fer-*

mata, a resting point, while at the same time being the conclusion of the cycles of discourse between the friends and Job.[6]

NOTES

1. On the discussion of this chapter, see Curt Kuhl, "Neuere Literarkritik des Buches Hiob," *Theologische Rundschau,* N.F. 21 (1953): 281–83.

2. Verses 15–20 are viewed by many as a subsequent addition because they "deal with a completely different theme." Indeed, v. 22 could smoothly and easily follow directly upon v. 14. But then one would have to regard the whole section vv. 13–20 as secondary—as Kuhl correctly observes, "since v. 20 once again takes up the theme of v. 12" ("Literarkritik," p. 282). What would then remain, however, would be a mere torso. From the explanation of the structure of the chapter as here given it becomes clear that the whole chapter has grown out of a series of expansionary processes. As a consequence of these processes, the two parts of this section do not totally coincide even though—as is probable—both these developments of the negative answer go back to the same tradition. Thus the discontinuity is explained from the structure, and neither vv. 15–19 nor vv. 13–20 are to be stricken from the text.

3. Thus N. Thilo (*Das Buch Hiob* [Bonn, 1925]) and A. Sietsma (*De zelfrechtvaardigung Gods: Zeven Preeken uit het boek Job* [Amsterdam, 1939], p. 75); cf. Kuhl, "Literarkritik," p. 282.

4. Cf. also Prov. 30:4; Eccles. 1:10; 2:12; 2:22–23; 6:12.

5. It seems to me quite certain that v. 28 is a secondary and deliberately corrective addition; thus Édouard Paul Dhorme (*A Commentary on the Book of Job,* trans. Harold Knight [London: Nelson, 1967] [= *Le livre de Job* (Paris, 1926)]), Samuel R. Driver and George Buchanan Gray (*The Book of Job,* International Critical Commentary 10, 11 [Edinburgh, 1921]), etc.; cf. also Kuhl, "Literarkritik," p. 283.

6. Thus also Hans Wilhelm Hertzberg ("Der Aufbau des Buches Hiob," in *Festschrift Alfred Bertholet zum 80. Geburtstag,* ed. Walter Baumgartner et al., pp. 233–58 [Tübingen: J. C. B. Mohr (Paul Siebeck), 1950]; Dhorme (*Job*); Helmut Lamparter ("call it 'halftime'" [*Das Buch der Anfechtung,* Botschaft des Alten Testaments 13 (Stuttgart: Calwer, ²1955), p. 163]); A. Lefèvre ("a moment of relaxation" ["Le livre de Job," in *Supplément au Dictionnnaire de la Bible,* ed. André Robert (Paris: Librairie Letouzey et Ané, 1949), vol. 4, cols. 1073–98]); W. O. E. Oesterly and Theodore H. Robinson ("a parenthesis" [*An Introduction to the Books of the Old Testament* (London: SPCK, 1953), p.171]); cf. Kuhl, "Literarkritik," pp. 281–82.

13

The Elihu Speeches

The extensive discussion concerning the position of the Elihu speeches in the Book of Job was based essentially on literary arguments, on the one hand, and on conceptual comparisons, on the other hand. In light of the current state of the discussion, these arguments have apparently not led to any firm conclusions.[1]

Even if the interpretation of the structure of the Book of Job as given here should prove to be accurate only in its broad traits, still that interpretation allows us to say with certainty that the speeches of Elihu are a subsequent addition to the Book of Job. These speeches are an insertion that could not have originated with the poet of the Book of Job; on the contrary, they quite obviously represent an early critical response to the Book of Job.

1. Already the introduction in 32:1–8 points out the secondary nature of these speeches. This introduction alleges that it takes up the disputation discourse where the friends have left it off. However, the dialogue section ends with chap. 23 (or chap. 27, if one includes the fragments in the dialogue section); Job's concluding lament in chaps. 29–31 is not a part of the dialogue. More important, the reason the friends stop speaking is misunderstood. Elihu becomes angry with the friends, "because they had found no answer and thus had put God in the wrong [cf. 32:3]." That is simply false; it is a mistake. The situation is rather that the final word on the part of the friends is the condemnation of Job (by Eliphaz, chap. 22), which intends precisely to put God in the right over against Job. It is simply false to say that the friends can no longer answer Job (32:5), if for no other reason than that chaps. 29–31 no longer stand within the disputational discourse. The fundamental misunderstanding of the Book of Job that has persisted even to the

139

present, namely, that it is the discussion of a problem, begins right here in the Elihu speeches.

2. A frequently advanced argument now appears in a new light: Elihu literally quotes clauses from the speeches of Job. After the excessively lengthy introduction, Elihu's first speech begins with such a citation in 33:8-11. Such a thing never happens in a real disputational discourse. The dramatic character of the Book of Job excludes the possibility of such citations from the very outset. This is no longer living dialogue; it has become literary polemic.[2]

3. The third and decisive reason lies in the very structure of the Elihu speeches. We saw that in terms of their structure the speeches of the friends are very carefully thought out and are composed of only a few motifs. The articulation of these motifs reveals a clearly recognizable gradation from the initial utterance of the first friend on up to the accusation in chap. 22. Only on the basis of the fragments in chaps. 24-27 does it appear as though the discussion simply goes on after this accusation, with repetitions of the earlier motifs. In reality the disputational discourse concludes, for the friends, with chap. 22 and for Job with chap. 23.

Following their strongly emphasized new starting point, the Elihu speeches go on to present a really different sort of speech, which comes to the fore most clearly in chap. 34.[3] This chapter is a lecture by a teacher of wisdom in a circle of the wise whom he addresses (34:2) and before whom he develops the case presented by Job, of whom he speaks in the third person. The conclusion once again expressly states that Elihu's real concern is the approval of these his hearers, before whom he has presented the case in question; the hearers must agree with Elihu that Job is to be reckoned among the transgressors (chaps. 34-37). Likewise, here in this speech the pretense is no longer maintained that we are dealing merely with an additional voice in the disputational discourse. This speech stands completely outside the scope of the dramatic event being played out among the friends, Job, and God; it is rather an objective, accompanying evaluation of Job's speeches. Moreover, the nature of this evaluation is very clear; the speech of Job (cited in 34:5-6) is condemned as sacrilegious, and Job is reckoned a transgressor (34:7-8). The material which then follows lays out the grounds for this judgment by Elihu. The judgment is once again repeated in the concluding section (chaps. 36–37), which summons the wise to concurrence in the judgment.

In terms of their structure the other components in chaps. 32–37 are recognizable only with difficulty and hardly at all with certainty. After the very extensive introduction which takes up the whole of chap. 32 (vv. 1–5 are a prose preface justifying the insertion of chaps. 32–37; vv. 6–22 are a speech by Elihu justifying his entrance), Elihu begins in 33:1 with an address directed to Job. It is very uncertain where this particular speech of Elihu stops and how the speeches that then follow are to be delimited. According to the superscriptions (32:6; 34:1; 35:1; 36:1), four speeches of Elihu follow one after the other. It soon becomes apparent that this introduction is a tardy attempt at tying together very disparate and confusedly assembled passages. One Septuagint manuscript has the beginning of a speech between 34:15 and 34:16. It is certainly true that 34:16, which is a calling upon Job to hear, belongs at the beginning of a speech; apart from that fact, however, such a speech is very unlikely in chap. 34, which otherwise speaks of Job exclusively in the third person. There is a second indication that this division of Elihu's speeches cannot be original. Job 33:31–33 is without doubt the introduction to a speech;[4] this speech is continued in 35:2ff. Thus chap. 34, the only really unified speech, has been shoved into the middle of another speech. In terms of their structure, both these speeches present difficulties which do not permit of solution. The Elihu speeches give the impression of being a rough draft that some later hand worked up into a series of four speeches, doing so in part very cleverly but in part with complete lack of understanding. One must add to this state of affairs the frequently insurmountable difficulties with the text, which is hardly so disrupted at any other place in the Old Testament as it is here.

In spite of all these difficulties, however, it seems to me that a schema for the structure of these speeches is recognizable, a schema which can bring at least some sense of order to these entangled texts. The starting point in this matter is the one quite certain difference shown by the Elihu speeches over against the other speeches of the friends: the Elihu speeches cite literally (or almost literally) clauses from the speeches of Job. Such citations include the following: 33:8–11; 33:12–13;[5] 34:5–6 (perhaps including the textually uncertain v. 9); 35:2-3. Only in chap. 33 can one clearly recognize the structure of an Elihu speech surrounding such a citation of a thesis of Job. This chapter begins with a calling upon Job to hear (v. 1), based upon a legitimatizing of the speaker (vv. 2-4). There follows the challenge to a disputation (v. 5, expanded in vv. 6-7 by means of a reference to the fact that Elihu stands on the same plane as Job). This challenge leads into the now following citation of the thesis of Job (vv. 8-11 and 12-13). Here we meet the difficulty that two different theses of Job are cited. Verses 8-11 contain an asseveration of innocence by Job (v. 9) and an accusation against God to the effect that God without reason treats Job as an enemy. Verses 12-13 contain, on the other hand, Job's thesis that God does not answer him. Only this second thesis is then disputed, and the disputation substantiated, in vv. 14-30. If we set aside one of these citations for the time being, namely, the one in vv. 8-11, then we get a clear, complete, and fully understandable structure: introduction— citation of a thesis of Job—disputing of this thesis.

The introduction consists of a call to hear (with a legitimatizing of the speaker, which happens only here and at 36:4) and a challenge to a disputation (with the expansion mentioned above). The main part of the speech is the disputing of the thesis of Job. Here in chap. 33 this disputing passes over directly (at v. 14) to a substantiating of the speaker's position, which is then widely developed (Job's thesis was that God does not answer; Elihu retorts that God answers in various ways [v. 14], and then he elaborates on how this answering of God takes place [vv. 15-28]). Verses 29-30 obviously form the conclusion. Thereby at least 33:1-30 is recognizable as a unified and intact speech of Elihu; the only difficulty is with the second citation (vv. 8-11).

This same schema can now be recognized, at least in part, in the other speeches which have been preserved intact.

A second speech begins at 33:31 with the calling upon Job to hear; in vv. 32-33 there follows the challenge to a disputation. Now one would expect the citation of another thesis of Job. This in fact comes in 35:2-3; after the removal of chap. 34, these verses follow directly upon 33:32-33. In 35:4 there follows the introduction to the disputation; this introduction differs from the one in chap. 33 in that it is directed to Job and his friends. The disputation proper is contained in vv. 5–8. (This much is at least possible, despite the fact that the context is not very clear. Job's thesis was "How am I better off than if I had sinned?" Elihu's rebuttal is that God is so exalted that the sins of mankind certainly cannot do *him* any harm; those sins can only affect other human beings.) Verse 9 is unintelligible following directly upon v. 8; there must be some textual disruption here. The substantiating of Elihu's counterthesis, which he draws into the fray against the position of Job, can only amount to a development on the theme of the exaltedness of God. Such a development is contained in another portion of the Elihu speeches, in 36:22–37:24. It is possible that this latter passage once followed directly upon 35:8. If one is unwilling to make this assumption, then one must rest content with the observation that this second speech of Elihu breaks off after the disputing of Job's thesis; 35:9–16 can hardly be viewed as the expected continuation.

The original sequence is even more difficult to recognize in the speech in chap. 36. The calling upon Job to hear is missing. We found such a call in the Septuagint at 34:16, where it was even tied in with the superscription upon which it would indeed have to follow. The Septuagint location of the call cannot be its original place, and thus it is quite likely that it belongs at the beginning of chap. 36.[6]

There follows the challenging to a disputation in 36:2–3, associated with the legitimatizing of the speaker in v. 4. Now one would expect the citation of a thesis of Job. Such a citation is missing, and yet there follows in vv. 5–7 the disputing of a thesis of Job. This disputation points out that God deals justly; he does not allow the wicked to live, but he exalts the righteous. The theme of exalting the lowly is then developed in vv. 8–15. One can perhaps infer the here disputed thesis of Job on the basis of Elihu's rejoinder; it must have been an accusation against God which maintained the contrary, namely, that God lets the righteous suffer without reason. That is precisely the content of the quotation of a clause of Job which we found in 33:8–11 and there characterized as being out of place. In other words, 33:8–11 probably belongs between 36:4 and 36:5 (whereby an immediately disputatious clause could have fallen out, for 36:5–7 begins as a substantiation). Now there still follows here a concluding section: an extensive admonition (vv. 16–17) and

143

warning directed to Job. The final warning clause in v. 21 is the conclusion of the whole.

The affiliation of 35:5-14 remains to be explained. Substantively this passage certainly belongs after chap. 33; it is a disputation of the thesis of Job that God does not answer him. This disputation has two sides: (a) God indeed answers, and to be sure in various ways (33:14-30). (b) If God does not answer, then man himself is to blame, since "only a transgressor does God not hear" (35:13a); God does not answer the wicked (35:9-14). Thus from a substantive point of view 35:9-14 certainly belongs with this speech in chap. 33. However, the location of this passage is not to be determined with certainty. It most likely belongs between 33:13 and 33:14, which is to say at the beginning of the disputation. It would also be possible after 33:30; however, vv. 29-30 sound very much like the conclusion of a speech.

Thus we find four speeches of Elihu, of which chap. 34 represents one type and the other three represent the other type. The structure of these Elihu speeches (except for chap. 34) is recognizable from chap. 33; the transpositions which are necessary on account of the doubtlessly disrupted text find their justification in the intact order of the first speech in chap. 33. On the basis of chap. 33 it is possible to recognize three speeches of essentially the same structure (see table below).

INTRODUCTION TO THE ELIHU SPEECHES: 32:1-3, 6-22

Calling upon Job to hear	33:1	33:31	[34:16]
expanded	2-4		
Challenge to a disputation	5	32-33	36:2-3
expanded	6-7		4
Citation of a thesis of Job	12-13	35:2-3	[33:8-11]
Disputing of this thesis of Job	[35:9-14]	4-8	5-7
Substantiation of the disputation	14-30	[36:22—37:24]	8-15
Admonition (and warning) directed to Job	35:14	(37:14-20)	16-21

The speech in chap. 34 agrees with this structure in one essential point: likewise here in the middle (vv. 5-6) there stands a citation of Job which is then extensively disputed. The disputation (vv. 10-12) is especially emphatic and elaborate. The substantiation follows in vv. 12-33 (without vv. 14-16). Thus we find the following agreement with the other three speeches: citation, disputing of the citation, substantiation. The introduction and the conclusion differ. Instead of the calling upon Job to hear, there is this same call directed to the wise as the hearers; instead of the challenge to a disputation, there is the resolution to discover and to actuate a judgment (in the case of Job). This judgment is already presupposed in vv. 7-8, following the citation of Job's own words; to a certain extent this judgment arises of its own accord if all one hears is the words of Job. Judgment is finally openly passed at the conclusion (vv. 35-37), to which the consent of the forum of the wise is presupposed (v. 34).

The overall agreement in the chief components coupled with the deviation in the conclusion and the introduction must catch one's attention. One gets the impression that in the other three speeches there is still a real conversation with Job; everything is still unresolved. Job can still be admonished and warned in the three speeches; they terminate in an extensive admonition and warning (36:16-21). In chap. 34, on the other hand, judgment is spoken upon Job before the forum of the wise; the whole chapter has about it the character of finality, of definitiveness. This impression receives additional confirmation when one compares the citations of clauses of Job in the other three speeches and in chap. 34. The other three speeches deal in each case with *one* thesis of Job or, as in 33:8-11, with two closely related clauses:

1. God does not answer me (33:12-13).
2. How have I benefited from not sinning (35:2-3)? (What is meant here is Job's thesis that God strikes the guiltless as well as the transgressor.)
3. Although I am innocent, God treats me like an enemy (33:8-11).

The citation of Job in 34:5-6, however, has a summarizing character: I am in the right—God has taken away my right—I must suffer despite my being in the right—My wound is incurable, save if I were guilty. To be sure, one cannot say that all the previously identified and disputed theses of Job are here once again summarized. Nevertheless, these brief clauses snatched from elsewhere do sound like a summation of the sacrilege uttered by Job. Unlike the situation in the other three speeches, we are not dealing here with a single statement of Job which is to be refuted. Instead we find here in chap. 34 the concentrated accusation which Job leveled against God: I am in the right, God is in the wrong.

If one now adds this observation to the preceding, one is thus in a position to venture the supposition that chap. 34 was originally thought of as the conclusion to the Elihu speeches. It is here in this speech that the conclusion is drawn; here is where it comes down to the final answer to the speeches of Job, the answer at which the friends did not arrive. Only now has Job really been proved in the wrong (v. 3b [*sic;* v. 35?]).

It thus becomes apparent upon close examination that only chap. 34 really corresponds to the intention of the Elihu speeches; certainly the intention is indicated clearly enough in 32:1–5. The starting point of Elihu has nothing in common with the starting point of the other three friends.[7] There is no mention of Elihu's coming to console Job; nothing is said of Job's bitter suffering. Only the *words* of Job interest Elihu; from the outset and without reservation he regards these words as blasphemy, because Job "considers himself more righteous than God." Elihu's anger, his zeal for God, is kindled by these words. In the same way, however, his anger is inflamed because in his opinion the friends have not given the necessary and clear answer *to the words* of Job. But in fact it is *only* in chap. 34 that this answer is so given by Elihu as to correspond to the heat of his wrath; only here is Job finally proven in the wrong.

Only now does the relationship of the other three speeches to chap. 34 become clear. These speeches are just what their introductions say they are: disputational discourse (cf. their structure). Job's case is discussed point for point (the citations). Job is even challenged to give rebuttal (33:5; 33:32–33); he is addressed, admonished, warned. None of this is any longer possible in chap. 34; the discussion is closed. The admonition and warning at the conclusion of the third speech (36:16–21) gave Job his last chance to express himself, which means in this context to retract his words (even though only in the sense of a literary fiction, as here). In the event that Job should remain silent,[8] however, judgment will now have to be pronounced against him. This happens in chap. 34.

Thus one can recognize behind the Elihu speeches a concept that is singular, unified, and in its own way impressive. This critique by Elihu is without doubt a later addition to the Book of Job.[9] It arose out of a true theological passion, out of a strong and deeply felt zeal for the righteousness of God. And in one sense this critique of the Book of Job is quite fitting and proper: If one understands the Book of Job conceptually, as a presentation of Job's *thoughts* about God and, along with that, the friends' *thoughts* about God, then the anger of a person zealous for the righteousness of God *must* be kindled at the words of Job; then the condemnation of the speech of Job *must* be carried out in a much more radical fashion than the friends accomplish; then the answering of the friends *must* be adjudged as in any case unsatisfactory. Aflame with righteous zeal, our critic who inserted the speeches of Elihu—naturally after the final, decisive cry of Job in which summons and petition merge—no longer says and was no longer in a position to understand that the utterances of Job are not a speech about God but rather a lament directed to God. Our critic no longer realized that he completely bypassed the *real* speech of Job when he took it upon himself to refute Job's most annoying statements point by point. A veritable abyss yawns between the place where the author of the Elihu speeches stands and the place where Job stands. Elihu simply *cannot* understand Job. Elihu's standpoint becomes clear in chap. 34: he speaks before the forum of wisdom, which exercises disposition over the standards of human speech about God and which, from its given standpoint, is in a position to condemn Job as a transgressor.

NOTES

1. Cf. once again the excellent synopsis of the discussion in Curt Kuhl, "Neuere Literarkritik des Buches Hiob," *Theologische Rundschau,* N.F. 21 (1953): 258ff. Especially valuable here is also the material in Édouard Paul Dhorme, *A Commentary on the Book of Job,* trans. Harold Knight (London: Nelson, 1967), pp. lxxvii–lxxviii.

2. Thus Dhorme, *Job,* p. lxxix.

3. The peculiarity of chap. 34 is recognized by Nichols (Helen Hawley Nichols, "The Composition of the Elihu Speeches," *American Journal of Semitic Languages and Literatures* 27/2 [1911]: 34–35).

4. Cf. the commentaries by Duhm and others.

5. Verse 12 is textually uncertain. According to the Septuagint translation it is a citation of Job; according to the Masoretic Text it is a combating of the thesis of Job as presented in vv. 8–11.

6. In chap. 34 the misplaced section that does not belong to the speech encompasses vv. 14 and 15 as well as v. 16; v. 17 certainly follows directly upon v. 13. If one takes 34:14–16 together and follows the Septuagint manuscript, which has a new speech begin with v. 16, then one would have in 34:14–15 the conclusion to the preceding speech. This agrees with our suggestion of having 36:22—37:14 follow upon 35:5-8. The result would be that the speech in question would develop as expected, namely, with the thesis of the majesty of the creator following the disputation in vv. 5–8, to which theme 34:14–15 would then fit excellently as a conclusion.

7. Thus also Kuhl, "Literarkritik," p. 258.

8. This eventuality is reckoned with in 33:33—and it is precisely at this place that chap. 34 ties in, with a certain substantive justification.

9. After a consideration of the arguments both pro and con, Kuhl also comes to this conclusion. See in this regard also the more recent interpretation of Möller, who sees in the Elihu speeches the solution to the Job-problem: "Elihu is—unlike the friends—the bearer of genuine divine revelation. . . . The Spirit of God compels him to untangle the threads which have gotten all interwoven in the disputational discourse. . . . The divine speech both continues and presupposes (!) the speech of Elihu and confirms it through its content" (Hans W. Möller, *Sinn und Aufbau des Buches Hiob* [Berlin: Evangelische Verlagsanstalt, 1955], pp. 96ff.). Given his premise, Möller arrives at general statements about the Elihu speeches which, despite Möller's best intentions, do not in any way reproduce what the texts themselves say: "In contrast to the friends . . . Elihu acknowledges Job's piety." Just read 34:7-8 and 34:34-37! In chap. 33 Möller hears overtones of the "Pauline-Lutheran doctrine of justification," whereby he bases his statement upon a debatable translation of 33:32.